WILDERNESS SEASONS

Life and Adventure in Canada's North

Ian and Sally Wilson

Illustrated by Sally Tatlow Wilson

Gordon Soules Book Publishers Ltd.,
West Vancouver, Canada

**With special thanks to Maureen Colclough
for all the hours, assistance,
and energy contributed to this book.**

First printing March, 1987
Second printing July, 1987

Published by
**Gordon Soules
Book Publishers Ltd.**
1352-B Marine Drive,
West Vancouver, B. C.
Canada
V7T 1B5

We wish to acknowledge the generous financial support
of the Canada Council in publishing this book.

Text © 1987 by Ian Wilson
Illustrations © 1987 by Sally Tatlow Wilson
No part of this book may be reproduced in any
form without prior permission from the publisher,
except for brief passages for the purposes of review.

Canadian Cataloguing in Publication Data

Wilson, Ian, 1955-
    Wilderness seasons

    ISBN 0-919574-34-3

    1. British Columbia - Description and travel -
1981-   *. 2. Frontier and pioneer life -
British Columbia. I. Wilson, Sally Tatlow,
1955-   II. Title.
FC3817.4.W54 1987   917.11'104   C87-091086-8
F1087.W54 1987

Contents

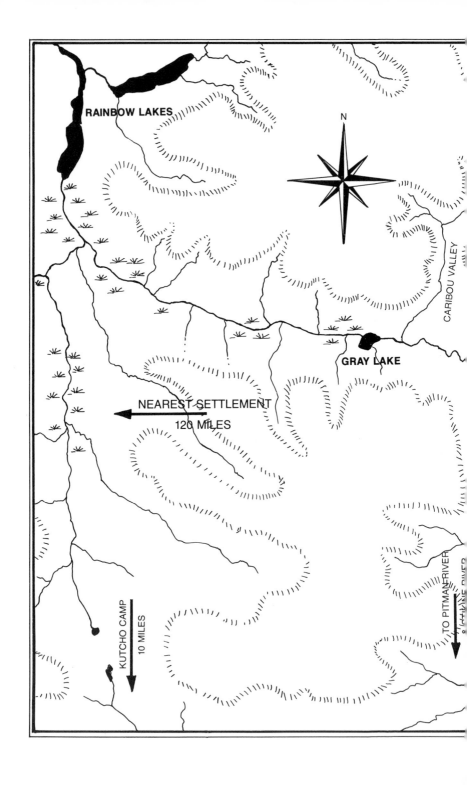

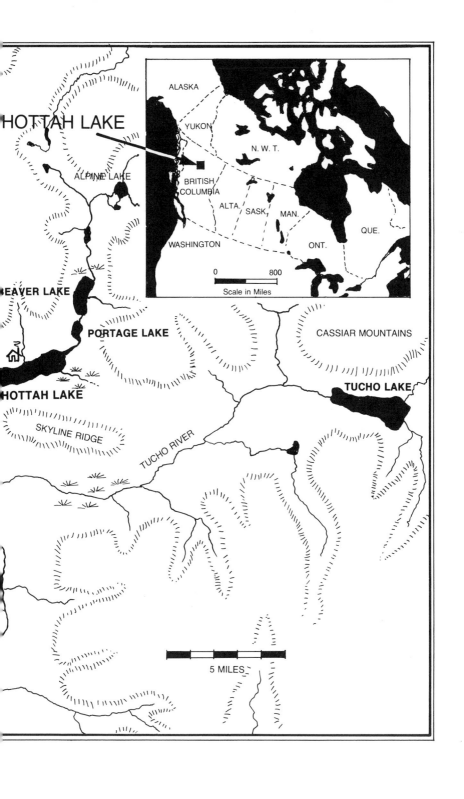

HOTTAH LAKE

ALASKA

YUKON

N. W. T.

ALPINE LAKE

BRITISH
COLUMBIA

ALTA. SASK. MAN.

WASHINGTON

ONT.

QUE.

0   800

Scale in Miles

BEAVER LAKE

PORTAGE LAKE

CASSIAR MOUNTAINS

TUCHO LAKE

HOTTAH LAKE

SKYLINE RIDGE

TUCHO RIVER

5 MILES

CHAPTER 1

Call of the Wild

Why would two otherwise rational individuals trade the comforts and culture of the city for life in a remote and uninhabited wilderness?

Sally and I have come up with many answers—but none of them seems to satisfy that question. Not entirely. Sally thinks it was the call of geese flying overhead one spring evening that beckoned us to follow them north. I feel it was the soothing sound of a gurgling creek by our campsite that made us realize we didn't want to return to the hectic city after our weekend outdoors.

We first shared our dream to live in the wilderness while we were sitting by a crackling campfire. As we silently watched the glowing sparks float into the darkness, I felt a strong sense of well-being, of belonging.

"Sally?" I asked tentatively, thinking that she had dropped off to sleep.

"Mmm?"

"Do you feel at home here?" I asked. "That this is where we belong, instead of rushing around the city all week just to get a day or two outdoors?"

Sally poked at the embers with a stick. Her auburn hair, entwined with bits of bark and grass, caught in the fire's glow and framed her tanned face.

"I feel comfortable here," she said slowly, "and closer to everything that I love. Today, when we watched those marmots basking on the rocks, I felt closer to nature—and closer to you." Sally sighed then continued, "We never seem to have time to talk in the city, to really share. In the woods we do."

Sally paused again. "I suppose it's just a romantic dream though. . . . "

"What is?" I said.

"You know . . . to live by ourselves somewhere, in a cabin in the woods."

There was a small smile playing about her eyes, a barely perceptible wrinkle, as if she knew what I was going to say next.

"We have it pretty good in the city," I agreed. "Good jobs . . . lots of friends . . . a nice home. But I've had the same dream for years—to live in a log cabin like the pioneers did when things were rougher . . . and simpler."

I sat silently, stirring the hot coals of the fire. Then, I took a deep breath and continued, "Maybe it's time we made our dream come true."

Sally stared into the fire for a long moment, her face turned away from me. "Maybe, but it's a big step," she said quietly.

By a kind of unspoken agreement, we let it go after that and talked about other things until the last embers of the campfire flickered out. It was as if we were afraid to discuss our dream any further.

Later, I lay in my sleeping bag thinking about our life in the city. Sally and I were in our late twenties. She had a successful career as a grain trader for a small firm, and I split my time between freelance photography and a regular job as a service manager for an automotive dealer. We enjoyed city luxuries, and city projects like fixing up our house. But we always felt pressured, hemmed in by crowds and cars, by bosses' commands and customers' demands. We suffered from stress and jangled nerves five days a week, and tried to recover by running off to the wilds whenever we could. It

7

was only outdoors that we were able to relax briefly, to be ourselves.

The outdoors had always been an important part of our lives, even before we knew each other. We loved skis and snowshoes, canoes and kayaks, backpacks, mountain trails and secluded woodland lakes. But we needed more than one or two days at a time to really become part of the outdoors. We were always just city people escaping for the weekend. Somehow, the balance seemed all wrong.

As we headed home after that weekend of discussing our dream by the campfire, we felt the pressures of the city more keenly than ever. On the highway the traffic seemed noisier, the pace more hectic. And as the streams of cars began to converge on the Lions' Gate Bridge, Vancouver's gateway from the north, we felt as though we were entering into battle. Somewhere in my inner ear I still heard the owl, softly hooting at us from deep in the forest the night before. That was where I wanted to be. I knew that Sally felt the same.

The calm that had been with me over the weekend outdoors seemed to dissolve in the hectic pace of the following day. As I rushed around photographing houses for a real estate client, I smiled grimly and remembered the words of Henry Thoreau, written over a century ago: "Why should we waste the best years of our lives earning money in order to enjoy a questionable freedom during the least valuable part?" These words still made a great deal of sense.

By early afternoon I found myself daydreaming of a quiet life, far from the fast pace and rat race, noise, and fumes. I closed my eyes tightly. For a moment I was walking towards a sunny clearing in the wilderness. A cabin was nestled there among tall trees on the shore of a calm, sun-dappled lake, and snowcapped peaks reached up to a brilliant blue sky. . . . The loud blare of a horn startled me out of my reverie. How I longed to leave the city!

On an impulse, I sought out a public telephone and dialed Sally's work number.

"Let's do it," I said.

"Do what?" she asked, teasingly. I could almost hear the smile in her voice.

"Get away from here. Let's go as far into the wild as we

can. The farther and wilder the better."

There was a brief silence. When Sally replied, she was almost whispering.

"When do we start?"

"Can you leave work a little early today?"

"Sure, but I'll have to buy a toothbrush if we're dropping out of civilization without stopping by the house first!"

I let out a quick laugh. "Maybe we'd better talk first, make a few plans. I meant, can you meet me at the library around three?"

"I'll be there."

I hung up, then dialed my client's office. Even though it was just past lunch time, I left a message that I was finished for the day, then climbed into my car. Within half an hour, I had picked up a collection of topographic maps of northern B.C. and was on my way to the downtown library.

The wail of a siren and a flashing light behind me made me swear under my breath. I suppressed my frustration as I pulled over.

"What's your hurry Mister?" a stern police officer asked as I rolled down the window.

I tried to explain. About my going to meet Sally with the maps, about making plans, about our dream of leaving the city noise and hustle behind. Then I stopped short. As the officer fixed me with a steely gaze, I realized that there was no way that I could ever make him understand.

Just then, a nearby jackhammer rattled off a string of mechanical expletives. We both grimaced. And suddenly the officer smiled.

"Good luck," he said with a wink, "and slow down!"

I did slow down, but my frustration with city life persisted. By the time Sally arrived at the library, I had papered an entire study table from end to end with maps, and secured them in place with stacks of outdoor magazines and books on wildlife, cabin building, and outdoor survival.

"What do you think of this lake? How about this cabin design? Look at all these wild plants we could eat. And...."

"Hey, just a minute!" Sally interrupted, laughing. "I want to go as much as you do, but it will take more than a few hours to plan our trip."

Sally and I spent the rest of the afternoon at the library,

poring over books, maps and aerial photographs. One of the first things we realized was that we would have to go north in early summer to have enough time to build a cabin before snowfall. When the library closed at nine o'clock we had amassed a pile of books and magazines to take home for further study.

At home that evening, we made a list of our requirements: we wanted a remote northern lake, near timberline in an open valley. I visualized a creek near our cabin, and accessible mountain peaks for skiing and climbing. We were also looking for an area with abundant wildlife to photograph and study, such as moose, deer, bear, mountain goat, wolf, and other wild animals. We hoped for good fishing, and a river that we could canoe back to civilization the second summer. As if all that weren't enough, Sally suggested that the lake should be located within one hundred miles of a float plane base, to keep down the cost of being flown in.

But most of all, we were looking for an area that was still wild, untouched by man.

It was a tall order. Finally, after two weeks of searching, I found a lake that seemed to meet all of our requirements. It was a mere speck of blue, hidden among the mountains, rivers, and forests of northern British Columbia. The nearest settlement was at Iskut, eighty-five miles to the west as the crow flies.

"This looks like it, Sally," I said.

Sally leaned over my shoulder and read the small print on the map, "Hottah Lake. Sounds good to me!" And that was how Sally and I picked the spot—sight unseen—where we would spend fourteen months in the wilderness.

We had found our paradise. On paper, at least. The next step was to break the news to our parents and friends.

"What would you think of two people selling their house in the city to homestead in the north?" I asked my mother casually one evening.

"Is this a hypothetical question?" she returned, with a twinkle in her eye.

"Well, maybe not," I admitted.

My mother paused for a moment, considering the question. I eyed her nervously, wondering if she would dismiss the idea as a foolish whim.

"It's not something I would do," she said, subconsciously pulling her sweater around her for warmth. "The idea terrifies me. But it sounds like the sort of crazy thing you would try. Not that I'm surprised, really. You've spent almost every weekend since you were thirteen traipsing into the woods!"

Perhaps my parents understood because they had lived in the Arctic for some years. Now they were supportive with ideas and many helpful suggestions. Sally's parents also understood the lure of an adventure. Her father's attitude was, "If it's what you really want, do it while you can!"

Our next-door neighbour's response was less encouraging.

"You'll give up the idea as soon as the first real estate salesman sets foot on your doorstep," he said. "You've put an awful lot of work into that house—painting, wallpapering, and all that copper plumbing. You won't want to leave it."

Two days later, in early May, our lawn boasted a large *For Sale* sign. Our plan was to sell the house quickly and save money by renting a cheap apartment instead of paying a mortgage. From the apartment we would organize our expedition.

Once our friends saw that we were in earnest, the kidding really started. We heard stories about man-eating grizzly bears, packs of wolves, and hordes of hungry mosquitoes—all these were rumoured to be in store for us in the north. The two most-asked questions were, "How will a couple of city slickers survive the cold winter?" and, "What will you two *DO* all winter in a tiny cabin?" This latter question was always followed by snickers.

Some thought we were crazy to leave our secure lifestyle and head for the wilderness; they had trouble imagining a life without urban comforts and conveniences. It would be a big step, leaving our friends and families behind, quitting our jobs, and selling our home—all for an uncertain dream.

Our closest friends understood our need to leave the city and shared our love of the outdoors, but to those who had to ask why we were going, we had no satisfactory reply. This need to seek out a simpler life was not something we could easily put into words.

11

For a long time it looked as though we would never escape the bonds of the city. Vancouver's housing market had gone into a sudden and discouraging tail-spin. Three months went by, and it was already too late in the summer for us to go north. The chance to pursue our dream seemed to grow even slimmer as four, then five months passed and no one offered to buy the house.

"Maybe we should let it stay a dream," I said to Sally after we had lowered the asking price for the fourth time. "The city's really not so bad."

Sally replied with a forcefulness in her voice that I had not heard before. "No, I won't give up . . . it's my dream too!" She knew it was what I wanted to hear.

We finally sold our house in October. Sally and I had mixed feelings as we turned over the keys to the real estate salesman and walked down the front sidewalk for the last time. We felt sad because we were leaving our first home. But we also felt a new excitement—now there was no turning back. Ahead of us was a winter of planning and preparing for our adventure. In seven months we would leave the city for a new life twelve hundred miles north, in a wild land of lakes, rivers, and forests.

As Sally and I stood on the walkway, we heard the faint honking of Canada geese. It was a good omen. We put our arms around each other and looked skyward to the graceful, southbound wedge of wings.

"They can pick us up on their way north next June," I said quietly.

CHAPTER 2

Planning and Packing

"Aren't you packing a toilet plunger?" my mother asked as she scanned the list of supplies Sally and I had drawn up for our fourteen-month sojourn.

I shrugged in mock exasperation. Other well-meant suggestions from friends had ranged from Honda generators to electric shavers. Obviously some people did not quite grasp the idea of our wilderness trip!

"Uh, Mom—we won't have a toilet in need of a plunger," I replied carefully, hoping that this wouldn't trigger a lengthy discussion of the comforts of the city.

"Well, a Maytag it ain't, but a plunger and bucket make a pretty good washing machine," she explained. A plunger was added to our twenty-page list of supplies, only to be questioned by almost everyone who read the list thereafter.

With the list in hand, Sally and I spent our lunch hours comparing prices of outdoor gear and trying to find insect repellant and mosquito nets in mid-winter. Every other spare moment was spent reading dozens of how-to books, on topics ranging from outdoor cooking and cabin building to winter survival. While our friends enjoyed weekends of skiing or hiking, we were occupied with courses on hunting, trapping, and first aid.

Even after all our reading, we had much to learn. As I nosed through the equipment at a camping supply store an old-timer began to quiz me about my outdoor skills.

"What's a greenhorn like you know about building a log cabin?" he asked.

"Not too much," I confessed.

"Have you ever used one of these ornery folding stoves before?" he questioned, poking a finger at my box of sheet metal on the counter.

"No," I answered. "But I'll learn fast!"

"Have you ever spent a winter up north?"

"Well, I've done lots of snow camping and backcountry skiing," I said.

The old fellow rubbed his stubbly beard and gave me a long look. "Well," he said, "what you don't have in knowhow, I reckon you make up for with gumption." Gumption, it seemed, was a most important asset for our adventure.

Unlike most expeditions, ours claimed the dubious distinction of having been outfitted at flea markets, secondhand stores and garage sales. Price was the deciding factor for most items—this was a budget adventure. We traded our small car for an old four-wheel drive truck and a trailer, and sold our household goods to buy building materials and tools, clothing, camping equipment and medical supplies.

After searching for many weeks, we finally found a used cabin tent at a second-hand store. The tent was in excellent condition, the correct size, the type we had in mind, and priced within our budget. There was only one problem—it was incredibly ugly. The roof and awning had broad, gaudy yellow and green stripes.

"It looks like a circus tent!" I protested as Sally and I inspected the canvas for any mildew or rot.

"So? No one will ever see it way up north anyway."

I finally conceded. We were in no position to turn down a bargain. "Besides, in an emergency we can always use the tent as a beacon," I added.

During the months of planning for our trip we constantly pestered friends and family for suggestions of items we might need to take. Our usual greetings to friends were replaced by, "Have you seen any good recipes for granola lately?" or, "How do you keep film from freezing at sixty below?" Where Sally and I were going there would be no hardware stores or grocery markets. We had to be fully self-sufficient. From sewing supplies to chainsaw parts, whatever we could not forage from the wild we would have to take with us.

One helpful lady who had lived in the north advised us of the need for mosquito nets, mosquito lotion and a "big gun" for protection. She then took Sally aside to divulge another necessity for northern winter survival.

"What is it?" Sally asked, fearing a serious omission on our list.

"A needlepoint kit," the lady gravely revealed.

Sally spent many evenings researching our dietary requirements for a fourteen-month menu. "Seems straightforward to me," I suggested. "Mars Bars, marshmallows and multivitamins should keep us going." For some strange reason Sally did most of the food planning without my able assistance, searching for menu ideas in outdoor and health food cookbooks, then using me as the unwilling taste-tester. Much to my consternation, I often heard her mumbling over breakfast about calories, cellulose and carbohydrates.

"What's this?" I asked glumly one morning, staring at a bowl brimming with a gummy grey substance. It was my fifth consecutive gummy grey breakfast.

"Porridge," Sally said brightly, as though the dish before me were a gourmet creation.

"What kind this time?" I had suffered through corn meal porridge, millet porridge, oat-grit porridge, and flax-wheat porridge with dried apple bits. This looked to me like rubber porridge. And I had never been a porridge fan, not even as a child.

Sally eyed me disapprovingly. "Just *porridge* porridge. You know ... oatmeal. Except that I added some mashed prunes and raisins. Breakfast is the most important meal of the day, and with only powdered eggs we won't be eating omelettes!"

I groaned, but tasted the porridge. It wasn't bad, actually. "I'll bet the pioneers never had to eat anything like this. What ever happened to beans, bannock and bacon?"

Sally laughed. We had been trying many new foods that we had never heard of before, including lentils, carob, and wheat germ. "Just wait until you taste what I'm making for supper—bulghur!" she said.

A coincidence that it rhymes with vulgar, I thought, but I prudently kept my comments to myself.

Over the course of several weeks, Sally drew up a twenty-eight day menu of nutritious, reasonably palatable foods, then multiplied the quantities by fourteen to arrive at the grand total we had to purchase. The list was staggering, and included three hundred pounds of flour, eighty pounds of rice, seventy pounds of oatmeal, sixty pounds of cheese, and twenty pounds of beans. I noted sadly that Sally had almost entirely ignored my suggestions. She'd listed only fourteen Mars Bars and one package of marshmallows.

While Sally figured out our food requirements, I completed an inventory of tools and other supplies we would need. To determine how much fuel to bring I spent one evening in our apartment burning candles, kerosene and Coleman lanterns, and a small gas stove.

As this strange procedure was under way, our paperboy came to collect his money.

His eyes widened as they scanned over the eerie array of glowing candles, hissing lanterns, flickering lamps, and a sizzling stove. With shaking hand outstretched, he quickly snatched his money and left without a word. As the paperboy ran down the hall, it occurred to me that the sight of axes, a maul, and two rifles lying on the floor may also have influenced his hasty departure.

I wrote letters to more than twenty companies detailing our adventure and asking for sponsorship. I asked them to supply us with goods; in return I offered photographs and reports on how the equipment performed. Many companies responded generously, and soon merchandise began to trickle in: a chainsaw from McCulloch, lanterns and fuel from Coleman, ski wax from Swix. Boxes were made specially for us by Domtar, Grumman supplied a canoe at cost, and Robin Hood gave us three hundred pounds of flour. Many other companies sponsored us with equipment or offered us goods at wholesale prices.

Our friends also sponsored our trip by buying raffle tickets for a chance to win a "wilderness week for two." This was a way of raising money, but we also hoped the winners would take advantage of the prize, which would be a trip to and from Hottah Lake with our supply flights in a small floatplane.

If only the government had been equally cooperative! We had to apply for a seemingly endless number of permits and licences: gun acquisition certificates, hunting and fishing licences, big game and waterfowl hunting permits, a radio licence, a land use permit, a licence of land occupation, and on *ad infinitum*.

"Wanting a simple life in the wilds seems to involve more paperwork than a small business in the city," I told Sally.

Our dealings with the Ministry of Lands were typically frustrating. Our first application was promptly lost, and from there it was all downhill. Another application and a month later, the forms were still being shuffled but not dealt with. More long weeks passed as this project was referred to the Ministry of Forests, the Ministry of Fisheries, the Ministry of Wildlife, and the Ministry of Water. My frustration mounted as I envisioned the mass of forms next going through a labyrinth of government offices such as the Ministry of Air, Inert Gases and Upper Atmosphere.

Still more weeks passed, and a drastic step was needed to speed up our application. The district manager for northern B.C. had not returned any of my calls, so I telephoned him at home on a Sunday night. This was bound to get action one way or another! I explained our problems and the fact that time was running out.

"Why do we need a mass of documents to live in the middle of nowhere?" I asked. "I've heard there are twenty squatters living near Dease River without permits."

For a moment I thought he had dropped the telephone. Finally, in a dry voice slightly tinged with annoyance, he assured me he would try to speed up the process.

We received verbal approval the very next morning. It seemed too good to be true . . . and it was. It took the staff another three weeks to type the documents. Then, with true government efficiency, the papers were lost again. After more anxious long-distance phone calls, we finally received our permits—only two days before we were to leave.

While we waited for our land-use permits we continued our other preparations for the trip. We bought cartloads of pancake mix, spaghetti and macaroni. From case-load sales and bargain days, we amassed a fourteen months' supply of toilet paper and canned goods. Our tiny apartment, which we had moved into after selling the house, began to resemble a warehouse. Boxes filled every available corner. Heaps of supplies piled higher and higher in the small living room and bedroom until we were forced to sleep on the floor, wedged between duffle bags, boxes and buckets.

"Well, at least we'll be used to living in cramped quarters," I said, shoving aside a pile of winter clothes.

Our last major task before we headed north was to buy and package the bulk food we needed. Imagine a weekly grocery cart multiplied by sixty weeks. The total came to fifteen hundred pounds! Sally and I spent three days bent over barrels scooping out everything from cornmeal to cocoa.

Once, as Sally was filling three enormous bags with dried apple rings, an inquisitive middle-aged lady peered across our overflowing shopping carts. As Sally twisted a tie around the third bag, the woman could no longer contain her curiosity.

"What in heaven's name are you going to do with all those apples?" she asked.

Sally smiled mischievously. "I'm going to make apple pies."

There was a long pause as the lady digested Sally's answer. Her curiosity still wasn't satisfied. "Do they make good pies?"

"I'm not sure," Sally said. "I've never tried them."

The lady surveyed the cart filled with bulging bags of dried apples, looked at Sally in amazement, then walked away shaking her head.

Our biggest shopping spree filled eight carts and two pallets. Sixty pounds of milk powder, forty pounds of granola, thirty pounds of honey, and rice in twenty pound sacks were among the items on the pallets. The overloaded shopping carts creaked and groaned under heaps of boxes and bags, and shoppers rushed to find checkouts ahead of our train of carts.

"We have a *very* large family," I explained to staring by-standers.

Mountains of bulk food piled up on our already cluttered floors. After purchasing all our supplies, we weighed, scooped, sorted, and divided each item into fourteen lots. I began to take on the flavour of our work as we poured sticky syrups, oil, and ketchup from large buckets into small containers. We acquired the essences of flour, pancake mix and milk powder as these fine dusts coated our sticky hands and clothing.

"I feel like I've been gastronomically tarred and feathered," I said, wiping my sticky hands on my pants.

The end result was a towering heap of almost three thousand pounds of food and gear: forty-seven boxes, twenty-two buckets, and an assortment of odds and ends including shovels, axes, a stove, skis and snowshoes.

"Are you sure this will all fit in our truck and small trailer?" Sally asked, dubiously.

I assured her that there was room for everything. Silently, I wondered if there would be. But everything did fit in —all except the stovepipes which I tied to the roof of the trailer, and two bags of bulky winter clothes which I stuffed in the canoe.

When we were almost ready to leave, we invited some friends over for a going-away party and the raffle draw. The winners were two friends I had worked with for eight years. Jim Dennis and Vern Jessen were delighted to accept the prize, and planned to visit us at Hottah Lake for a week in late August.

"Can you think of anything that's missing?" Sally asked as our friends eyed the huge pile of gear.

Most just shook their heads. "It's so cluttered in here, I wouldn't notice if Ian was missing," one person quipped.

On the sixth of June, 1983 we were finally on our way. With a rather overloaded truck and an old trailer wagging behind us we left the city to follow our dream. I'm not sure which feeling was stronger—excitement at beginning an adventure, relief that the hectic months of planning and packing were over, or apprehension about what lay ahead.

"Look up," Sally said suddenly, her voice filled with excitement. Overhead, a flock of Canada geese was going our way. We began our twelve-hundred-mile drive north.

But only two miles down the road, our trip ground to a halt, when we noticed clouds of black smoke billowing from the trailer.

"Great start!" I groaned. Fortunately, the smoke was caused only by a fender that had come loose and was rubbing against a tire. A twist of wire repaired the sagging fender and we continued on our way.

Our drive north to Iskut proceeded without further incident until we reached the dotted section on the map marked "gravel road", one hundred miles from our destination. This road was rough and dusty, but passable until large impressive signs informed us of road improvement projects. These signs invariably signalled an obstacle course of construction equipment, ruts, mudholes and large potholes.

I shuddered every time we saw one of these signs. They always seemed to precede the worst stretches of road, and at one point we had to shift into four-wheel drive to negotiate a muddy stretch. A mile before our destination an exceedingly large crater caused a spring to part company with the trailer. Somehow, we limped into the small settlement of Iskut. We arrived, caked with a liberal portion of "improved" road—just one day before our pilot was scheduled to fly us into the wilderness.

Sally and I checked into a campground, and soothed road-weary muscles under the last hot shower we would have for the next fourteen months. Refreshed, we went to a small roadside restaurant to enjoy what we jokingly called our "last supper." We revelled in juicy burgers, cold beer and ice cream—treats made more delicious by the prospect of long months of deprivation ahead.

It wasn't surprising that we couldn't sleep that night, but passed the time talking about the coming events. In less than twelve hours we would be flown eighty-five miles deep into mountain country to a remote lake which we had only seen on maps and aerial photographs. We had travelled twelve hundred miles north in search of wilderness, left the comforts of the city for the rugged life of pioneers, and more than seven months of preparation were behind us.

"I sure hope our lake will look as good tomorrow as it has on paper these last months," Sally whispered.

CHAPTER 3

Civilization to Solitude

Our heartbeats quickened as the drone of the Beaver floatplane grew louder. Blue-and-yellow wings flashed in the sun as the plane banked and roared low overhead. A plume of white water rooster-tailed behind the floats, then the plane settled onto the lake. As it taxied towards us I felt the same mixture of excitement and trepidation I had felt as a youngster, waiting in line for a roller coaster ride.

From the cockpit, our pilot gave us the thumbs up sign and a broad smile. Then he brought the bobbing plane to a crunching halt against the wharf.

"Sorry I'm late—had to glue a wing on," he grinned, tossing a rope to Sally. Ron Bruns was a quiet, wiry northern bush pilot with a perpetual twinkle in his eye. He was said to be one of the best pilots in the area.

Ron walked around our pile of gear and lifted a couple of boxes to check their weight, then studied the large pile to estimate the volume of our supplies. Finally, he leaned against the plane and pushed back his grease-stained cap.

"Is this one load or two?" he asked casually.

I was dismayed. We had planned our loads carefully so

they would be brought in by four flights through the summer. We had calculated the exact weight of our supplies for each flight. We had even arranged for Ron to store the gear until it was flown in. But, we had apparently misjudged the volume of the plane. The interior of the floatplane was considerably smaller than a van, and tapered to a space only two feet high at the back.

We began jamming boxes and bags into the aircraft. I wondered which of our belongings we would have to leave behind, to be squeezed in with another load.

"Do you really need those two suitcases where you're headed?" Ron asked, with a puzzled expression. When I told him that they contained valuable camera gear he shrugged his shoulders and tossed another box into the plane. I grabbed the two cases protectively and gently placed them behind the passenger seat. I would leave a box of food behind if necessary, but not the cameras!

Our woodburning stove was a real challenge to load. Ron and I wrestled the 150-pound bulk over the edge of the dock, and rested it on one of the pontoons. We paused for a moment to consider how to get the unwieldy object over the door frame of the bobbing plane.

"I'll go inside and you push it through the door," I suggested.

Sally and Ron heaved and shoved the stove up the ladder to the door, and finally pushed it into the plane. Sally sighed with relief when the stove was safely stowed. Then, as Ron lifted the stove door, I cautioned, "Watch the handle, it's loo—." But it was too late. The handle came off and the fifteen-pound steel door splashed into the cold lake.

"Well, who's ready for an early morning dip?" Ron asked, as Sally peered into the grey water. Fortunately, the door had lodged just below the surface, between the dock and the pontoon. Sally reached into the water and quickly retrieved the door before the plane bobbed away from the dock.

"That was close," she said.

It was a tight squeeze, but we managed to pack all the boxes, bags, and bundles into the small plane. Sally climbed in the back and wedged herself between boxes, then we piled clothing and packs on top of her. I sat up front, perched on a cardboard box; I was the expedition photographer, and made the most of the excuse.

Flying in the small floatplane was like being on a wild carnival ride with eight hundred pounds of food and equipment packed around us. I thought the old plane would rattle apart as we roared down the choppy lake.

"Quite a load!" Ron yelled over the engine noise as we neared the end of the lake. At what seemed to be the last possible moment, the plane lumbered off the lake and became airborne, barely skimming over the shoreline trees. I distinctly remember seeing one tree that appeared to be only a few feet below the floats, and wishing that I was with Sally in the back of the plane, where the view was obstructed by boxes and duffle bags.

As Ron looked over the valley below, and pointed out landmarks and lakes, I could tell that he enjoyed flying. We left behind us the last vestiges of civilization that Sally and I would see in a long while. Roads, buildings and telephone poles gave way to spectacular snowclad mountains, bright green valleys and braided silver rivers. Ron followed the broad valley of the Stikine River, then coursed along the winding Pitman River.

The scenery below was breathtaking. Mountain peaks closed in as we flew up the narrow ribbon of water which Ron confirmed was the Tucho River.

"You going to canoe that?" he shouted over the engine noise, pointing to an ominous looking stretch of boiling water.

"Well, we might have to walk part of it," I shouted back. I thought to myself that the aerial photographs had made it look so easy.

I watched nervously as we headed straight for a mountain ridge, then abruptly climbed and flew what appeared to be only a few feet over the top.

"Worth the price of admission alone," Ron boomed with a wicked grin. After nearly an hour of flying, we travelled up a narrow valley and descended to "our" lake. Ron circled the lake as I referred to the aerial photographs.

"That's it!" I shouted, pointing to a small creek on the north side.

Ron pulled back on the throttle, almost stopping the engine as we skimmed over the water. I gripped the edge of the seat with white knuckles as the lake rushed up to meet the floats, then shuddered as the plane bounced onto the water.

"Great landing," I smiled weakly as the plane roared towards a sandy beach. As soon as the engine stopped I climbed out and onto firm ground and breathed a sigh of relief.

"Sure is quiet here, after that plane ride," I couldn't help commenting. The clear lake water slapped rhythmically against the floats, and the call of a jay drifted from the forest as I absorbed the spectacular view.

A thumping noise from inside the plane broke my reverie, and a muffled voice called, "Hey, let me out!"

Sheepishly, I extricated a white-faced Sally from the pile of gear.

"I was sure you'd forgotten me," she said, then stretched her legs which were cramped from being squeezed between boxes.

"There's nothing but a wobbly latch holding the rear door closed," Sally said. "I spent the entire flight holding the door shut, expecting it to fly open and the boxes to fall out at any moment!"

"Oh, it's always been like that," Ron reassured her. "Haven't lost anyone yet . . . at least I don't think I have."

Sally and I stood on the sandy beach and shared our first impressions of Hottah Lake. It was a breathtaking view. The sun glittered on the small emerald-green lake, which reflected a mirror-perfect image of lush green forests and tall, snow-capped peaks.

Ron pretended to busy himself with a mooring line as Sally hugged me tightly. "It's beautiful," she exclaimed. "Just as I hoped it would be!"

We unpacked our gear on a beach where perhaps no person had ever stood before. Suddenly, in these surroundings, our pile of supplies didn't look so very large any more. Ron took a last look at the jumble of boxes and bags, shook his head, and wished us luck.

"I'll make a note in the log book as to where I left you . . . Jeff or I should be back in a week or two with your next load," Ron said as he climbed into the cockpit. No sooner had he settled into his seat than he leaned his head out and pointed to the sand. "By the way, those are bear tracks," he said, and started the engine.

Sally and I stood quietly on the beach, holding hands until long after the drone of the plane faded. I hugged Sally close as the full impact of our situation hit us. Hottah Lake was all that we had dreamed it would be. But we suddenly felt very alone, far from the safety and comforts of the city. I wondered what challenges lay ahead for us in this remote land. Could we survive in this wilderness, with the nearest help over eighty-five air miles away?

"This is it," Sally whispered. "No turning back now."

Silence . . . solitude. Nearby, a soft gurgling stream led through a rock garden of forest flowers and moss-carpeted boulders. The forest behind us exuded fragrances of sun-warmed pine needles and wildflowers. The surface of Hottah Lake sparkled like a thousand jewels strewn across a glass table, and serrated peaks towered all around us. Our eyes followed the rocky shoreline around the lake to a majestic mountain at the west end. This beautiful valley was to be our home for the next fourteen months.

We desperately wanted to explore this wild, welcoming land, but we had work to do first. The most important task was to cache our food away from animals. In a country populated by grizzly bears, wolves, and wolverines it was important to keep food away from camp. Our safety depended on it. Even porcupines, martens and other small animals could be a nuisance if attracted by the presence of food. We suspended the canvas bags of food from a high branch of a tree, out of the reach of animals.

We covered the rest of our supplies, then I couldn't wait any longer to go exploring.

"Let's have a look around and see what we've got ourselves into!" I said.

We set off through the forest in search of a site for the cabin. We selected first one place, then another.

"How about this?" I asked as we found a small sunny break in the pines.

"Too steep," Sally said judiciously. "What about that grassy meadow?"

"It might flood in the spring," I replied.

Finally, we found the ideal cabin site, only half a mile

from our cache. It was a small level clearing near a whispering stream and sheltered by pine trees. The site faced south overlooking a sandy stretch of lakeshore. We pictured our front window looking out over the lake to the mountains beyond, and quickly agreed this would be the location of our cabin. Later, we discovered that this was precisely the location we had pinpointed on the map when we began planning our trip, many months before.

We hiked back to our campsite, set up our small tent on the beach, and lit a fire to cook a late supper. The excitement of the last few days finally caught up with us as we rested wearily by the campfire. But, the crackle of the fire, the scent of pine, and the soft whisper of wind in the trees had a soothing effect. As Sally and I watched the ever-changing images in the glowing coals, we felt the sense of well-being that came to us only in the wild.

"I almost can't believe we're here," I said quietly to Sally as she leaned her head against my shoulder.

It was after ten o'clock when the sun began to dip behind distant peaks, painting the sky crimson and gold. As daylight slowly faded, squirrels chattered and scolded and the lonesome call of a loon echoed across the lake. From somewhere deep in the forest came the long, low howl of a timber wolf. I thought of the popular notion of the silent north, and smiled.

We crawled into the tiny tent, and settled down contentedly in our sleeping bags for our first night in the wilderness. I teased Sally to keep an ear tuned for grizzly or wolf growls, but she coolly shrugged off my warning with a nervous laugh.

"Goodnight," she said firmly, then blew out the candle and wriggled down into her sleeping bag.

There was a brief, dark moment of silence. Then Sally suddenly shrieked, leapt up and started thrashing about in the tent. I fumbled about in the dark, taking a few blows to the ribs from Sally's flailing limbs before finding and lighting the candle.

"There's something in my sleeping bag!" she yelled.

A small furry field mouse had found the bed first, and had run up Sally's leg. Pandemonium followed as we chased the scrambling mouse around the cramped tent.

Our first night at Hottah Lake

A friendly neighbour

I finally managed to clap my boot over the frightened creature.

"Open the door!" I ordered.

When Sally opened the tent door to shoo the errant mouse away, we looked up into a pair of enormous brown eyes—a curious moose was only ten feet from the tent! We stared at our second visitor in awe. A moose is a huge animal, even to a viewer who is standing upright. To a reclining viewer, looking at a moose from the ankles up, the animal is positively gigantic.

"Gee, he's ugly!" Sally whispered.

The young bull moose had a long hairy nose, large droopy lips, and a drape of skin which dangled unappealingly under his chin—a face only a mother moose could love. Patches of fur had fallen out as he shed his winter coat, and long spindly legs made him look ungainly and awkward.

The moose eyed our little shelter with interest, but showed no sign of fear or aggression. He stood placidly for a while, munching on willow shoots as though assessing this new development in his neighbourhood, then slowly wandered down to the lake.

We no longer felt alone in the wilderness. The north was our new home, and our neighbours couldn't have given us a better welcome.

CHAPTER 4

A New Life

On our second day at Hottah Lake we awoke to mixed rain and snow with howling winds. Sally unzipped the tent door to peek outside and a cold gust of wind tore the tent flap from her hand.

"It's your turn to make breakfast—I cut the kindling last night," Sally remarked as she zipped up the door and crawled back into her warm sleeping bag.

"Just my luck," I grumbled. I unrolled my rain jacket which had served as my pillow, found a pair of slightly stiff socks under my sleeping bag, and forced myself out of the dry tent.

"I'd like my pancakes golden brown, and my syrup warmed," Sally called after me.

Torrents of rain poured down upon my breakfast preparations while Sally remained dry in the tent. I set up our folding Yukon stove, carefully arranged kindling, firewood, and a few wood shavings in the stove box, then struck a match. The pelting rain extinguished the flame before it even reached the shavings. I tried again, shielding the match with my body and gently blowing on the pile of shavings.

The damp kindling wouldn't light. I added more shavings, which burned merrily for a fleeting moment, then flickered out.

"What's taking so long out there?" Sally called from the comfort of her sleeping bag.

My reputation as a woodsman was at stake. I had been a boy scout; I had taught wilderness survival courses; I could start a fire in the face of any adversity! It was time to resort to the Flash-Wilson firestarting technique.

I located a small cylinder among our supplies and splashed a little of its contents over the kindling. I tossed in a match, threw on the lid, and leapt back. BOOM! With a thunderous roar, the stove erupted into flames. Fire darted from every crack; black smoke belched from the stovepipe. Then the stove collapsed into a heap of steaming metal.

"What happened?" Sally shouted as she scrambled out of the tent and ran to the disaster site.

She quickly surveyed the scene and spotted the metal cylinder. "Did you use white gas?" she asked in a voice edged with concern and irritation. Sally disapproved of my unorthodox firestarting techniques, and there was no point in trying to dodge the question. My singed shirtsleeve and the smoldering carcass of the "folding" Yukon stove gave me away.

"Needs a couple of screws to hold it together," I mumbled. My patience had run out. "*You* try to light a fire in a mickey-mouse folding stove, using wet kindling, and with rain pouring down!"

Sally made a barely audible comment about "woodsmen," then deftly started our small gas stove. Breakfast was a pot of camp coffee and cold granola with milk made from powder and water.

"If this is summer, winter should really be something," I said as water dripped from my sou'wester hat into my coffee. Until we had a tarp shelter set up, we had no choice but to eat in the rain; if we ate inside, the scent of food would almost certainly invite wild animals to the tent.

As soon as our soggy breakfast was over we dove back into the tent to wait out the heavy rainstorm.

"Not exactly what I had in mind for our second day in paradise," I exclaimed.

"Oh, I don't mind a quiet day after the excitement of the past week," Sally replied, as we snuggled in our zipped-together sleeping bags and listened to the drumming of rain on the roof of the nylon tent.

When the clouds finally lifted late in the afternoon, we were surprised and a little shocked to see the mountain peaks blanketed in new snow. Perhaps winter was not quite over in the north. Snow still lingered five hundred feet up the surrounding mountains and lay in shady hollows in the forest. The lake had been ice-covered only three weeks earlier, and the night air still carried a chill which made a warm campfire welcome.

Sally and I spent the afternoon and next day setting up a temporary camp for the summer. I headed into the forest to cut poles for our eight-by-ten-foot canvas tent while Sally cleared an area by the lake . . . right in the middle of a game trail. Through the day, I had stumbled across moose and bear tracks, an abandoned set of caribou antlers, and the remains of willow shoots that had provided a snack for some animal.

"Great spot for a tent," I remarked dryly after surveying Sally's work. "Sure hope a moose doesn't crash into our tent on his way home one night!"

We set up a tarp for our cooking and eating shelter two hundred feet away as a precaution against animals being attracted too close to the tent. The large plastic tarp over a framework of poles would be our kitchen, living room, and workshop for the next two months; and a rustic shelf of peeled poles would serve as a workbench and kitchen counter. An up-ended metal box made an adequate kitchen table, and on either side of it we placed two rounds of wood as chairs.

Our third evening brought a beautiful sunset, lighting up the western hemisphere as if it were on fire. Pink cotton-candy clouds floated in the sky, and brilliant splashes of red and orange illuminated the dark, rugged peaks. We stood quietly at the lakeshore, hand in hand, enjoying the colourful sunset and our wilderness. Suddenly, a loud rustling came from the underbrush.

"What's that?" I whispered nervously. There was an ominous growl in response, raising the hair on the back of my neck. A massive grizzly bear emerged from the bushes only one hundred yards from us. It walked several paces towards us, stood up, and sniffed the air. The bear swung its head from side to side and growled menacingly. The huge animal was so close that I could see every feature of its dark angry face.

"Don't move!" I hissed to Sally. I needn't have said anything—Sally was not about to budge. I stood motionless, one hand gripping the handle of an axe which had been beside me. The bear's deep growls and the bristling fur on its shoulders warned us that he was not happy about our presence—this was *his* territory.

The grizzly bear was the animal we feared most. This was our first encounter with the animal scientists had labelled *ursus horribilus*. Although grizzlies live mostly on berries and small rodents, they can be unpredictable and aggressive. As I stared at the large animal, I remembered stories of bears attacking large mammals such as deer—or people. My thoughts flashed back to newspaper accounts of unprovoked grizzly attacks on hikers, and I contemplated just how far we were from any help. Whatever happened, we were on our own.

An eternity seemed to pass as we stood frozen with fear. Finally, uttering a few last threatening growls, the bear turned and tromped back into the forest.

"I was going to get him with the axe," I said weakly. We were both trembling; we kept straining our eyes towards the dark forest, sure that the grizzly would return.

The thin walls of our canvas tent offered little comfort to us that night. Every time we heard a twig cracking in the forest we imagined that it was the bear rummaging around our camp. For the first time since arriving at Hottah Lake our decision to live in remote wilderness seemed a little reckless—there were so many dangers in our new life, and so much to learn about the north.

The very next morning we began building a permanent animal-proof food cache away from camp. I thought that perhaps the scent of the food sacks swinging in the trees had attracted the bear, and we decided our first priority was to store the food as far away as possible from our living quarters.

We decided upon a food cache design, similar to the type that Yukon trappers had used years ago to keep their supplies out of animals' reach. First we needed to find a group of four trees in a square formation, about six feet apart. After much searching and a discussion of the merits of a triangular cache, we finally found four trees in a rough rectangle.

We built a long ladder from poles, then I climbed it to trim the branches off each tree to a height of twelve feet. Next, I stood on the top rung of the shaky ladder and prepared to top the first tree. Using the chainsaw while perched precariously twelve feet above the ground was a risky job. As a safety precaution I tied the ladder to the tree, and the chainsaw to the ladder. My suggestion that Sally steady the ladder while I cut the tree did not meet unanimous approval.

"I'm not standing underneath a falling tree!" Sally said, backing away.

"This should be quite a ride!" I hollered, then started the chainsaw. Slowly, carefully, I cut into the tree. I glanced down twelve feet to the ground below, and fervently hoped the top would fall away from me.

"TIMBER!" I hung on to the ladder with all my strength as the tree top started to fall. The tree, and the ladder—with me on it—swayed violently from side to side as the tree top crashed to the ground. I held on tightly until the swaying stopped, then with my knees trembling and heart pounding wildly, I slowly descended the ladder.

"I think I'll take a break before tackling the next one," I said in a shaky voice.

Sally watched with apprehension while I climbed the ladder to top the next tree with the whirring chainsaw. It was a one-person task, and Sally found it almost as nerve-racking to watch as I found it to execute.

After I had topped all four trees, we notched and hoisted two heavy crossbeams into place across the tops of the standing posts. Small poles laid across the beams served as a floor, and a tarp stretched over a framework of poles would protect our supplies from the rain. As a final precaution against animals climbing up for a free lunch, I tacked sheets of aluminum around each support post. We were now

The food cache

Chef of the day

The cook shelter

prepared for the planeload of food and supplies which we expected our pilot to bring within the next week.

There is no sleeping pill like a good day's work outdoors. We collapsed into our sleeping bags and fell asleep almost as soon as our heads hit the makeshift pillows of clothes. Had I ever thought that sleeping on a thin foam mattress on the hard ground was uncomfortable? We slept more soundly than we had ever slept in the city, and only woke when the sun flooded our tent with warm yellow light the next morning.

I rolled out of my sleeping bag and drew in a breath of cool mountain air. From the tent door, I watched a sleek brown beaver swimming in the misty lake and heard the clear *pee-weet weet* of a spotted sandpiper as it ran along the shore.

It was my turn again to light the fire, coaxing wood shavings into flame before adding kindling and larger wood. Having finally mastered the mysteries of the Yukon stove, I enjoyed the rituals of starting the day: strolling down to the lake to fetch water, making coffee, and cooking breakfast. After some time the aroma of camp coffee mixed agreeably with the pungent scent of wood smoke, luring Sally from the tent.

After a leisurely breakfast, I convinced Sally that it was too nice a day to work. It didn't take much coaxing, and we decided to take the day off to climb the 5700-foot mountain behind our camp. Even though it was a warm morning, we packed rain gear, warm clothing, a first aid kit, and a large lunch; we knew that mountain storms and cold winds could come unexpectedly.

Willow and birch shrub were dripping with morning dew as we started up the mountain. Underfoot, spongy sphagnum moss, soft and saturated with water, cushioned our steps. Long wisps of green lichen hung from branches like the beards of old, old men, and white bunchberry blossoms carpeted the forest and sprouted on decaying logs, giving the woods a fairyland appearance.

Glimpses of the lake spurred us higher through the thinning forest. We were still wary about bears after our recent encounter and kept an eye out for them as we traversed a meadow of red heather. Suddenly, a loud thumping noise came from a group of stunted windblown trees. We froze in our tracks. Then, a spruce grouse flushed up right in front of us with a loud whirr of wings. I'm not sure who was more startled and frightened: Sally, me, or the grouse!

These grouse are called "fool hens" because they will remain motionless and allow a person to walk up to them before moving. Their camouflage was so effective that three more hidden grouse flew up from under our feet as we continued.

Sally and I climbed higher up the barren, windswept mountainside. From the top we enjoyed our first panoramic view of an area we had only seen on maps and aerial photographs. Two thousand feet below us lay the emerald-green jewels of Hottah Lake and two unnamed lakes to the east, perfectly proportioned and set in rings of dark evergreens and lofty peaks.

Hottah Lake stretched three miles from east to west and one mile across. Through binoculars we could see our tiny camp situated halfway along the north shoreline, beside the creek we had followed up through the forest. At the east end of the lake was a bottle-shaped inlet where a white blur of fast water foamed through a narrow canyon. At the west end, Hottah Lake drained into the Tucho River—a gleaming platinum ribbon winding through narrow valleys to join the Pitman and Stikine rivers.

Farther to the west was an open valley where a patchwork quilt of auburn willows, beaver ponds, and green marshes flowed across the landscape. On the southern horizon lay the broad flat plain of the Spatsizi Plateau and endless rows of peaks stretched as far as the eye could see. Looking over the vast expanse, we could see no sign of man, only a beautiful untouched landscape of forested valleys, mountains, lakes and rivers.

I gazed longingly at the rugged majestic peaks, knowing that few had ever been climbed. This was our "mountain high," our inebriation.... We were intoxicated by the landscape. Our feeling of well-being came from the heart-pounding exercise of climbing to the peak and the awe-inspiring natural beauty around us.

"I wonder if anyone has ever been up this mountain before?" Sally mused as we rested on a large, sun-warmed boulder. It was an interesting thought to consider; perhaps we were the first people ever to see this view. We sat silently, absorbing every feature of the untouched wilderness. Sally and I felt small, overwhelmed by the immensity, but strangely quite safe in the mountains—more at home here than we had ever felt in the city.

We hiked down through the forest as the afternoon sun slanted through lacy dark green branches. A squirrel chattered from a nearby tree, and the hollow tap-tapping of a woodpecker echoed in the forest. Sally and I walked in silence, entranced by the sounds and beauty of the forest around us.

"This is why we came to the wilderness," Sally said.

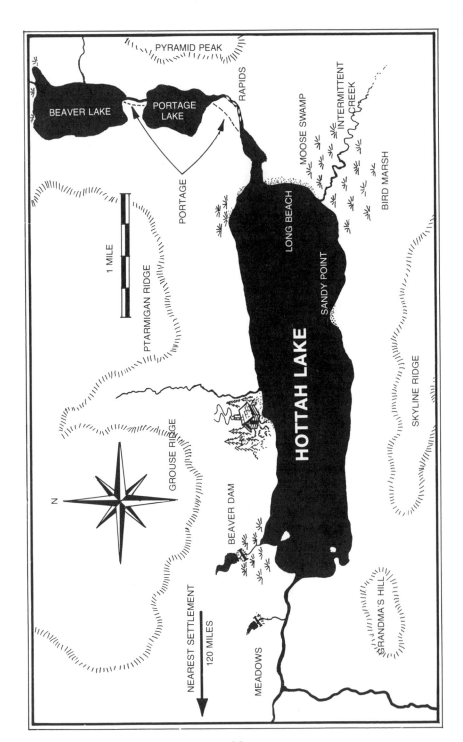

PYRAMID PEAK

BEAVER LAKE

PORTAGE LAKE

RAPIDS

PORTAGE

INTERMITTENT CREEK

MOOSE SWAMP

BIRD MARSH

LONG BEACH

SANDY POINT

1 MILE

PTARMIGAN RIDGE

HOTTAH LAKE

SKYLINE RIDGE

N

GROUSE RIDGE

BEAVER DAM

GRANDMA'S HILL

NEAREST SETTLEMENT

120 MILES

MEADOWS

CHAPTER 5

Wilderness Homestead

Many years ago, northern pioneers cleared small homesteads and built log cabins. More than anything else, it was the challenge of hewing a home from the forest that had lured Sally and me to Hottah Lake.

The first step to carving our homestead from the wilderness was to clear the land of tall willow and birch shrub. Even though the site we had chosen was a level area with no trees, preparing it took two days of cutting, sawing, and hacking at the tangled mass of bushes with axes and a bucksaw.

Once we had cleared the cabin site, I was prepared to take a day off and rest my tired muscles. But Sally had other plans.

"To be true homesteaders, we have to plant a garden," she insisted. Although I didn't share Sally's expectation of a bountiful harvest, she fully expected me to share the work of digging the garden.

"Summer nights here go down to just above freezing," I protested, "and the birds will munch on our seeds."

Sally nodded knowingly.

"Animals will graze on our crop," I continued, thinking I had settled the discussion.

Sally just shrugged and handed me a shovel.

Within a few minutes I found myself digging a four-by-six-foot plot behind the cabin site while Sally carried bucket loads of humus from a nearby marshy area and collected rich, dark soil from the base of trees. After turning this into the sandy garden we planted rows of beans, peas, lettuce, cabbage, and carrots. I teased Sally about the garden, but secretly hoped that the long summer days would yield fresh vegetables to supplement our supplies of dried food.

By late evening Sally and I were exhausted, covered with dirt and sticky sap, and our backs ached terribly. As quickly as we could, we washed in the cold lake, then lit a campfire to cook supper.

"How do you like pioneer life so far?" I asked, after we'd wolfed down a meager meal of bannock and cheese.

"Beats nine to five!" Sally replied. "But I'd sure like a hot bath," she sighed, inspecting her stained and blistered hands.

Since our arrival at Hottah Lake we had only taken quick dips in the lake—very quick dips. It was much too cold to consider lingering for a full bath. Tonight, a makeshift shower by the campfire seemed to be the answer, and with great anticipation we heated a pot of water.

"This is going to be great," Sally exclaimed as I stood on a stump, ready to empty the bucket of hot water over her head.

Sally's delight was short-lived; mosquitoes came from miles around to join in the festivities. It was like a slapstick comedy as Sally simultaneously showered, dodged smoke from the fire, and swatted mosquitoes. Then she frantically dried off and scrambled into her clothes.

It was my turn next. I don't recall ever having showered faster. Spurred on by hungry mosquitoes biting at normally unexposed parts of my anatomy, I undressed, showered, swatted at least fifty mosquitoes, dried off and dressed—all in less than two minutes!

Sally's laughter had just subsided after my shower dance when she started to giggle at my next performance. It seemed that even the simple act of shaving was first-rate entertainment. I must confess that I had never used a razor blade before. In the city, I had used an electric shaver, and each of my previous forays into the woods had been an opportunity to grow a stubbly beard.

In addition to the tribulations of learning to shave with a razor, I faced another problem: the day after our arrival we had broken our only mirror. I had to peer into the tiny sighting mirror of a navigation compass. My facial contortions and sharp intakes of breath added a touch of drama to the otherwise mundane task of shaving, and Sally's fits of giggles did little to help my concentration.

"Ouch!" When I had drawn blood for the fifteenth time, I decided to begin growing a beard immediately.

The thought of a bristly beard disturbed Sally more than me, but the one luxury I missed in our new life was a comfortable place to contemplate the day's events. What we needed to build next was an outhouse with a view of the lake.

I never imagined that designing and building an outhouse could be so exciting and challenging! This was our first attempt at putting up a log structure, and we tackled the project with boundless enthusiasm.

Cutting down the small trees for the outhouse was not as difficult as I had thought it would be—although I have to admit I cheated by pushing the trees in the direction I wanted them to drop. I knew this method would not work with bigger trees, but my confidence grew with each one that I felled. I looked forward to tackling the larger, cabin-sized trees.

Our first attempt at notching wall logs was not quite as successful as cutting them down had been. Like the pioneers, everything we did was by trial and error. The first few rounds of the outhouse fitted poorly and were crooked, but corner notches and logs fitted more closely as we gained experience measuring the notches and working with the chainsaw and chisel.

"It's just an outhouse!" Sally protested when I insisted that we carefully measure and fit each wall log.

"I know, but at thirty below in a howling wind you'll be thankful we notched these logs properly," I replied.

The result of our labours was a slightly lopsided but decidedly comfortable pine throne. Thinking of the rains to come, we tacked a sheet of plastic over the pole roof.

Two days of building with logs had taught us more than any how-to book could. We figured we had made all our mistakes on the outhouse and now felt ready to fell larger trees and to work on our log home.

Finding a safe place to store the toilet paper was the final, but most important part of building the outhouse. Some of our furred neighbours had rather strange gastronomic tastes, and we had already found that toilet paper was one of their favourite snacks. My brilliant solution was to suspend the roll from the ceiling on a string.

"This will keep varmints from munching on our TP," I assured Sally.

Sally's howls of laughter the following morning brought me running to the outhouse. A breeze in the night had unfurled yards and yards of our valuable tissue onto the floor. To add insult to injury, a mouse had chewed the mass of precious paper to bits. I conceded that Sally's idea of using an old coffee can with a tight-fitting lid, though not as picturesque, would be more effective.

Between building projects, camp chores kept us busy. So busy, in fact, that we sometimes wondered how we would ever be able to build a cabin before the end of the summer. Often, entire mornings passed while we split firewood, washed laundry, or baked. In addition, we had our tools to sharpen or maintain: the chainsaw was my responsibility, while Sally looked after the axes, machete and other tools.

"What have you been splitting with this axe—boulders?" Sally muttered as she toiled over our bush axe with a file and whetstone in an effort to remove large nicks from the blade.

"As a matter of fact, I have hit one or two," I admitted. It was almost impossible to avoid hitting the occasional rock while we were chopping branches off felled trees, and consequently the bush axe required constant filing.

We always left the big task of laundry for sunny days, so the clothes could dry on the line. First, we heated water on our Yukon stove—hardly the most efficient device for heating the gallons of water needed for the job. It was a challenge to get our odd assortment of pots and buckets crowded

Cutting notches

An airy pine throne

A view to the west

onto the stove. Whenever the fire needed stoking, we had to remove several precariously balanced pots, and lift the lid to add pieces of wood. Then, we carefully put the pots on top again.

After almost two hours of heating the water, we began the washing. Sally would drop a bundle of dirt-stiffened laundry into a bucket filled with clean, hot water. The toilet plunger was the agitator, and I was the human motor.

"Ninety-nine . . . one hundred!" I would count, announcing the end of the wash cycle. After two more buckets of clean water, and another two hundred plunges, the rinse cycle would be completed.

Our clothes had absorbed a great deal of local colour; the black pants I had been wearing finally returned to their original blue colour after three washings in hot water to remove pine sap, plant stains, and dirt. To do a washing that one would normally toss into an automatic washing machine took us almost half a day, from heating the water to hanging the clothes to dry.

Canada jays perched on one clothesline, chickadees rested on the other, and a mouse chewed a corner of a towel which I had draped over a bush to dry. With all the attention our laundry was attracting, I had visions of a moose trotting through the hanging tangle of clothes and running off with the multi-coloured product of our wash day streaming from its antlers!

While I did the laundry, Sally baked muffins for the first time in a collapsing reflector oven placed in front of an open fire. This "collapsing" oven was in the same class as our "folding" Yukon stove. To regulate the temperature in the oven, Sally would move it closer or further away from the heat of the fire. Unfortunately, the slightest bump made it fall apart.

"Hope you don't mind a few pine needles in your muffins," Sally said as she scooped half-cooked muffins off the ground. Without this marvelous contraption we might never have known what a real upside-down cake was! But even though the oven collapsed occasionally, we found it was a valuable aid to camp cooking.

A few days later, Sally found that bread baking outdoors had its own special problems. She did everything according to the recipe: kneading, punching, and rolling the dough on a rough plank that I had cut with the chainsaw, then setting the bread in the warm sun to rise. But she hadn't counted on a curious weasel trampling and sampling the dough before it rose.

"Get out of there!" I heard Sally shout, then watched as a brown streak of bounding weasel ran by, closely followed by Sally waving a wooden spoon.

"I'm not baking bread for thieving animals!" Sally shouted after the retreating animal.

The old northern substitute for bread was bannock, made by mixing flour, water, baking powder and lard. Bannock could be fried, baked, roasted, or even wrapped in foil and tossed in a fire, and it became our mainstay for the summer until the cabin was built.

Other visitors around camp were not quite as bothersome as the weasel. The small, red-backed field mouse that had visited us on our first night in the tent became our mascot and kept the kitchen tidy by cleaning up crumbs from the counter. The mouse's fur was a soft rusty-brown across the back and light grey underneath. Two shiny black eyes sparkled from an expressive face and black whiskers twitched on the end of a long pointed nose.

Even though the little mouse chewed towels and gloves and gnawed on my boots, we enjoyed its daily visits. We would observe its quick, nervous movements as our bold friend nibbled a morsel of food or scrubbed its face and whiskers with tiny paws. Each day our camp visitor became bolder, and eventually the small creature would clean up our plates as soon as we had finished eating.

One afternoon, a sudden thunderstorm blew in and I rushed to grab my rubber boots. As I picked up a boot the little mouse scampered out—with a mouthful of yellow felt lining.

"Almost squashed the little beggar!" I laughed as I surveyed the damage to my boot. Down in the toe was a small nest of yellow wool and a cache of food. I removed the nest and placed it under a tree, hoping the mouse would take the hint and find new premises.

The rainstorm later forced us to seek shelter in our tent. Strong westerly winds whipped the lake into rows of foaming waves, a loud continuous roll of thunder echoed through the valley, and heavy rain pounded on the roof of our flapping canvas tent. This was a summer shower—northern style.

Around seven-thirty in the evening we detected a muffled drone amidst the noise of the storm.

"Do you hear a plane?" Sally asked. We had been expecting our second supply flight for a few days, but I couldn't imagine our pilot flying in this weather.

"It's just the wind," I replied, but as the drone became louder we scrambled into our rainsuits and ran to the beach. We watched with astonishment as Ron's small floatplane flew up the valley, skimming between low clouds and the treetops.

Gusts of wind-driven rain swept down the lake and large waves crashed onto the shore. Buffeted by the strong wind, the plane circled three times, then finally flew low over the lake and splashed onto the turbulent water.

"I thought he wasn't going to land!" I shouted to Sally.

Ron brought the plane roaring straight towards shore, then cut the engine, jumped onto a float, and threw me a rope before the plane could blow away.

"Great day for flying," Ron commented as we helped him unload the plane.

Ron had brought in a planeload of supplies, which included our emergency radio, and food to last us until the end of the summer. As the pile of gear grew on shore, I wondered aloud how he had squeezed it all in the plane.

"No problem," he declared. "Oh yeah, almost forgot something." Ron opened a hatch in the left float and pulled out two five-gallon cans. Our chainsaw fuel! I shuddered to think of the consequences if he had not remembered those cans.

Ron politely declined our offer of a tour highlighting our log outhouse. "I'd better be going, the weather looks like it might get bad," he said in his typically understated manner.

"Don't forget that you're bringing in Jim and Vern on the next flight," I reminded Ron as he climbed into the plane.

As the floatplane took off unsteadily into the wind, I realized that we might not see anyone until Ron returned with our next supply flight, in two months. With the exception of the small radio, our last link with civilization disappeared into the clouds. Once again we were completely alone.

Sally and I busied ourselves with the task of carrying food boxes to the cache to keep our minds off what we were both thinking. Ron's visit reminded us of the world we had left behind, and we felt our solitude more keenly now than when Ron had first brought us to Hottah Lake.

Reading letters in the tent that evening made us a little homesick for the city. We wondered if cutting ourselves off so completely from friends and family had been a wise decision. Could we really live for fourteen months without the social contact which had been so much a part of our former lives?

As we discussed our feelings, the rain slowed to a soft patter and the sounds of the forest began to break through: the watery whistle of a thrush, the musical chorus of the chickadee, and the sassy chatter of a squirrel.

We went to the beach and stood for a long time, sharing the sights and sounds of our wilderness world. Low evening light shone through a break in the clouds and a muted rainbow arced across the east end of the lake. We watched as the sun slowly passed between the clouds and horizon with a last flush of crimson, then faded to burgundy as it dipped behind the high mountains above Hottah Lake.

Slowly, we came to understand that we had made no mistake. This was home.

CHAPTER 6

Timber!

"I'll show you how to cut down trees," I said confidently as I sharpened the chainsaw.

"Okay," Sally replied. "But I'll watch from a safe distance, thanks."

Bolstered by this vote of confidence I studied a log-falling manual then headed into the forest, armed with the chainsaw, axe, and falling wedges to cut down my first "big" tree.

I remembered the instructions from the manual: "Cut a V notch half way through the trunk on the side you want the tree to fall towards. Then, from the opposite side, cut down to this notch. As the tree begins to fall, shut off the chainsaw and move to a safe location." No problem. I had the instructions memorized.

In practice, I found the trees indeed fell in the approximate direction I intended, but seemed to fall towards any object within range, as if drawn by a magnet.

"Good shot, deadeye," Sally remarked as the first tree I cut down missed my intended mark by thirty feet. On my next attempts I was able to score direct hits on a small tree, a stump, and once in the branches of a standing tree. After more practice my aim improved, with only a few notable and spectacular exceptions.

According to my estimate, we would need four large logs for the base of the cabin, twelve logs to be cut in half lengthwise for the floor, thirty logs for the cabin walls, six for the gable ends, and three sturdy roof beams. We decided not to cut any trees around the cabin site, but to leave them standing for protection against cold winter winds. By cutting trees in scattered locations out of sight from the lake we hoped to have as little impact as possible on our environment. Each tree that we cut would be fully used, either for cabin construction or winter firewood.

We tried to choose logs approximately ten inches in diameter at the base, tapering to eight or nine inches at the twenty-foot mark. Lodgepole pine trees were abundant in the area and they seemed ideal for cabin building. They grew straight, with few branches and only a little taper. But even the best of them weren't perfect. I was amazed that trees which had looked so good while standing seemed to develop curves, grow branches, and gain other defects as they fell.

Once I had cut down a tree, Sally chopped the branches off with an axe while I measured and cut the tree to length. Then, using the edge of an axe, we loosened the sap-laden bark and used a peeling spud (a sharp edged tool which I had made from an old shovel) to scrape off the bark. But we soon found that the easiest method to peel the bark was simply to grab a strip and pull!

Cutting and peeling the logs was easy compared to the task of hauling them through the bush to the cabin site. Sally and I worked side-by-side, pulling on a length of chain and straining every muscle. It was backbreaking work, and we sometimes felt that we were little more than draft horses.

"Pull!" I urged as we wrestled our first three-hundred-pound log through the forest. Each time the front of the log dug into the ground I felt as if my shoulders were being pulled out of their sockets. When our combined efforts weren't enough to budge the stubborn log, we used a small hand winch called a come-along. We winched the log sideways, then continued pulling . . . slowly, tediously toward the cabin site. We managed to pull a grand total of two logs to the cabin site that day.

Two days later my patience had run out. "Dammit," I cursed when my right forearm muscle knotted into a cramp. "We've only hauled five logs to the clearing. There must be a better way."

"I've got it!" Sally said brightly. "How about floating the logs down the creek to the lake, then towing them right to the cabin site?" I had to admit that it seemed like a pretty good idea—anything was better than sweating and cursing a log through the forest.

We selected the largest and most difficult log, and dragged it to the creekbank. Without too much difficulty, we were able to tumble the log down the slope. We watched smugly as it bobbed merrily down the creek . . . for all of ten feet.

The log then came to an abrupt, grinding halt when it lodged between two large boulders in the middle of the icy creek.

"Any other brilliant ideas?" I laughed. Sally glared at the log and sat down in disgust.

Because it had been raining all morning, I had a notion that we couldn't get much wetter by trying to rescue the log. I was wrong. What followed could be best described as a Laurel and Hardy routine: we slipped and slid on the moss-covered boulders as we pulled, pushed, and rolled the un-cooperative log down the rocky waterway.

"Ah-h-h!" I heard Sally scream as her boots shot out from under her and she splashed sideways into the creek. I scrambled over to help her, plunging into the water. As we stood up to our knees in the near-freezing water, fighting our way back to shore against the swift current, it occurred to me that pulling heavy logs through the dry, warm forest wasn't such a bad idea after all.

That night, we went to bed absolutely exhausted. The muscles of our arms, backs, shoulders and stomachs ached from the strenuous work. As Sally and I massaged each other's sore muscles, we discussed other ways of bringing logs to our homestead.

"How about if we haul the logs downhill to the lake, then

tow them behind the canoe to the cabin site?" I suggested.

The following morning Sally agreed to try my idea. We canoed along the north shore of the lake to a stand of pine trees, and hiked up a steep slope. As I began cutting a large tree I confided knowingly to Sally that trees always fall uphill.

The tree crashed downhill only minutes later.

"Trees always fall uphill, do they?" Sally said. This phrase became a rather overused joke in the following weeks.

Despite a few errors, my skill at felling trees improved each day. I took more time to determine the lean of a tree, chose trees with a clear falling path, and used plastic falling wedges to guide the direction of any difficult trees. As with most tasks, I found that skill came with practice, not from reading a book.

Pulling the slippery, peeled logs downhill was easier than any other method we had tried, but on the steeper hills it was sometimes difficult to determine whether we were pulling a log or it was pulling us. The logs slid uncontrollably downhill until they wedged in a hollow or bashed into a tree, then we would have to wrestle them free and start them on their way downhill again.

Towing the large timbers behind the canoe also proved to be more tricky than we had expected. It seemed the wind always changed direction only minutes after we started canoeing up the lake with our heavy load. We would inch our way along the shoreline, slowly paddling into the wind and waves.

"It still beats dragging them through the bush," Sally said, puffing between paddle strokes.

We used our hand winch to haul the logs up the steep bank to our clearing, then we stacked them in a criss-cross pattern to air-dry. Once dried, they would be lighter and less likely to warp.

For three weeks we collected logs from different locations. Each log took almost two hours to find, fell, delimb, peel, then haul to the cabin site, and the pile of logs grew slowly. Fortunately, the northern days were long. Daylight brightened the sky by three in the morning and lingered until eleven o'clock at night, inspiring us to work long hours.

Peeling a log

Sally hauling a log

Towing logs to the cabin site

The hard work and long days gave us almost insatiable appetites. We consumed two or three times what we had eaten in the city, and nibbled constantly on trail mix and bannock between meals. Sally had calculated a plentiful diet of fifty-five hundred calories per day for each of us during the working months, but we still lost weight.

Each morning we checked the progress of our garden, dreaming of the day we would be able to dine on fresh vegetables. We did our best to chase away the pine siskins and other birds that feasted on the seeds or stole the beans' support strings for their nests. Deer also came by to check out the garden, but a tin plate in the breeze kept them at a distance. Within a few weeks we were rewarded by the appearance of tiny green shoots.

Sally began to plan menus: "stir-fried pea pods, fresh carrots, and salads with oil and vinegar dressing."

But one afternoon while I was sharpening the chainsaw, Sally came running from the garden with bad news.

"The peas—they're gone!" she cried, hauling me towards the garden to see. Some creature had come by in the night and eaten the entire crop. Tracks in the soft earth indicated that the suspect was a rabbit gourmand with a taste for something different.

"If I ever find that varmint, he'll be rabbit stew," I vowed. The rest of our meagre crop consisted of only small sprouts and assorted weeds.

Although our garden was a disaster, there were many wild edible plants in our valley and we learned to live off the land much as the pioneers had. Blue violets, rich in vitamins A and C, blanketed the open forest. We used the pale-blue petals to adorn our meals, and the glutinous leaves made a tasty soup when simmered with powdered milk and water. Fireweed, when boiled in salted water, was a good substitute for fresh vegetables. The young stalks were considered a delicacy by French Canadian settlers who called them "asperge", or wild asparagus. We found many other edible plants and berries to supplement our meals, and looked forward to a late summer harvest of blueberries, crowberries, and currants.

Our meals were simple and nutritious, but with the same staples to work with week after week, it became a real challenge to create new and interesting recipes. On our lazier days, we fished for rainbow trout, but we longed for a more varied diet, especially for crisp salads and fresh milk.

As we worked in the forest, I often teased Sally with descriptions of unobtainable treats such as juicy hamburgers or ice cream sundaes. No detail was overlooked as I expounded on the magnificence and flavour of these foods. The more Sally groaned, the more descriptive I became. Sally would retaliate with mouth-watering word pictures of fruit salads, strawberry shortcake garnished with whipped cream, or other tantalizing treats.

Food was an important part of our outdoor life, especially on rainy days when bannock and jam and a thermos of hot tea made the cold, wet weather more bearable. During one heavy downpour we sat under the dry sheltering branches of a large spruce tree to wait out the storm. As we sipped our hot tea, a pine squirrel scampered over to share our snack. The squirrel darted back and forth from the safety of the tree, coming closer to our food each time. We threw a piece of bannock to our small visitor and watched as he nibbled on the treat and turned it over and over in his deft hand-like paws. His chirring noises and nervous antics kept us entertained until the storm had passed.

The weather usually determined our activities each day. When it rained we pulled on rubber boots and rainsuits and worked in the forest felling and peeling trees. But on the few sunny days the lure of beautiful scenery took us from our work to explore our remote valley.

One sunny morning I suggested we dismiss work in favour of exploring the lake. As the canoe slipped through the still water, we surveyed the scenery around us. We felt like early explorers paddling into new country. In our remote area few landmarks had names, so we began the enjoyable pastime of naming each mountain. A deceptively easy looking peak to the west which, as Sally suggested, "even my grandmother could climb," was dubbed Grandma's Hill. We named a majestic, pointed peak to the southeast the Little Matterhorn for its resemblance to the Swiss mountain, and a towering triangular mountain at the east end of the lake became Pyramid Peak.

We canoed west along the shoreline, then detoured up a

small creek in search of beavers. We knew they were in the vicinity because we had spotted fresh willow and birch cuttings along the shore. As we canoed further up the creek we saw the pointed stumps of small spruce trees which had been cut down by beavers.

"I wonder if they have any better luck predicting the direction of fall than you," Sally teased.

We paddled quietly up the creek, enjoying the scenery and warm morning sun. Suddenly, a loud splash on the water shook us out of our reverie.

"What th— !" Sally shouted as she jumped in surprise. A narrow canoe is not the ideal place for sudden movement. Jumping up is definitely not recommended. Sally's reaction to the loud noise almost tipped us into the creek.

As we laughed about being startled by a beaver, a small black nose surfaced nearby and tiny black eyes peered about. We remained motionless as the beaver swam towards us with his soft satin ears perked up and nose quivering in the air. About six feet from the canoe the animal caught our scent, and slapped his broad flat tail on the water again, splashing us as he dove. After a minute or two he resurfaced and swam behind the canoe, accompanying us for some time before heading back down the creek.

Around the next corner was a long, curved beaver dam almost one hundred and fifty feet across, holding back a large pond. Beaver dams are an engineering marvel— convex-shaped for strength in deep water, and straight for shallow ponds. The dam was a convenient bridge for many animals, and we found tracks of wolves, porcupines, martens and other small animals in the soft mud.

On the far side of the pond sat a five-foot high dome-shaped beaver lodge built of earth and twigs. We hauled our canoe over the dam and paddled to the lodge. Sally climbed carefully onto the lodge and put an ear to a ventilation hole.

Sally listened for almost ten minutes, and was just starting to become restless at her post when I noticed a stream of air bubbles rising to the surface of the pond. The bubbles continued to the lodge and I guessed that a beaver had gone inside. Then, Sally motioned for me to join her. Through the air vent I could hear a faint squeaking.

"There must be babies inside," I whispered excitedly.

We took turns listening, thrilled at this opportunity to hear young beavers. If we had been in a hurry we might have missed this wonderful experience.

While canoeing back to camp, we talked of how our life had changed since moving to our remote valley. Our new life was simple and rugged, with none of the luxuries we had been accustomed to. But we considered our closeness to nature to be a special reward. Each day brought us not just the obstacles and frustrations of felling and hauling trees, but new discoveries.

We now took the time to smell the flowers, to listen to beavers in their lodge, or to watch the changing colours of a sunset. Time no longer had the same meaning that it had in the city and our days were no longer divided by hours and minutes. I had stopped setting the alarm or wearing a watch. Instead, we woke with the sun, ate when we were hungry, and went to bed when we were tired.

We had learned a special lesson during the five weeks we had been at Hottah Lake—we had learned to slow down.

CHAPTER 7

One Log at a Time

Sally and I stood in the clearing, looking at the jumbled pile of fifty peeled logs which had taken us the entire month of July to collect. In front of us, four corner stakes marked where our wilderness home would rest.

I had always felt confident that we could raise our own log cabin. But now, as I held a pencil sketch of a cabin in one hand, and a how-to book in the other, I felt overwhelmed by the size of the project.

"I'm not sure whether the hard or the easy part is behind us," I confessed.

"Remember what that old-timer in Iskut said when I asked how he built his cabin?" Sally responded.

The grizzled old trapper had shared words of wisdom that seemed to be a good philosophy for cabin building as well as for life. I smiled, then slowly repeated his words, "How do you build a cabin? One log at a time." By worrying about only one log at a time, the project no longer seemed so overwhelming.

The structure we had in mind was a traditional Yukon trapper's log cabin, with a low pitched roof that extended over a front porch. The walls were generally built just high enough for comfort, but low enough to conserve valuable heat from a small woodburning stove. Most front doors opened inward to keep the occupants from becoming snowed-in. We planned our cabin to be a sixteen-by-eighteen-foot version of this time-tested design, which had proven its worth in a land of long, frigid winters.

Our limited experience in building the airy outhouse, and a guide to log house building were all we had to go by. I turned to the first chapter of the guide and read aloud, "The first step is to build a level, sturdy foundation."

"I could have told you that!" I laughed. We prepared a level foundation of sand and gravel for good drainage, then we dragged four of the largest logs to the cabin site to serve as base logs. But then we were stumped. We knew we had to notch and place the base logs, but the manual neglected to show us how to line them up squarely without using elaborate tools. Fortunately, Sally and I had already learned that improvisation was an important part of wilderness life. After puzzling over the problem for a considerable time, I thought of using our navigation compass to aid us in lining up the logs.

Sally sighted along each log with the compass as I shifted it into position, and then we pegged them in place. By the next afternoon we had positioned and notched all four base logs, with the side logs lying due north to south, the front and rear logs east to west.

It took three more days to cut floorboards for the cabin. Each pair of floorboards had to be painstakingly sawn from a log, following a chalk guideline. It took me almost an hour to work the chainsaw down the length of each log, and I had to sharpen the chainsaw before starting to cut another floorboard. After that experience, I would never take a smooth, level floor for granted again!

"No wonder most trapper's cabins had only dirt floors," I muttered, as I strained with the chainsaw down the length of another fifteen-foot log.

I consoled myself with thoughts of the pioneer days of handsaws and hardships, when settlers had used six-foot whipsaws to cut green logs into planks. Sawing planks was a gruelling two-man job in those days, with one man pulling the saw from above and the other from a pit below. Unable to see his partner, each would accuse the other of not doing his fair share of work. While the man on top strained in the hot sun to pull the heavy saw up, the man in the pit was showered with woodchips, sawdust, and obscenities. We at least had the advantages of using a small chainsaw, of being able to see each other working, and of suffering slightly fewer flying woodchips and obscenities.

After we'd cut twelve of the straightest logs in half lengthwise, we laid them flat side up on a ledge cut into the base logs. Sally trimmed between the floorboards with an axe and I hewed rough spots with an adze, then we pushed a block of wood under each board to prevent it from sagging. Our workmanship steadily improved, from lumps, bumps and gaps at the back to a reasonably level floor with few gaps at the front.

"Too bad the cabin isn't four feet longer," I said. "By the time we were at the front it would be perfect."

"I like it just the way it is," Sally replied, looking at the gaps between the logs. "We'll be able to sweep any dirt down between the floorboards!"

With the floor completed, we began the first round of wall logs, putting into practice skills we had learned by building the outhouse. Sally and I lifted the first wall log into place, then carefully measured and marked each corner to be notched.

We used a simple square notch to join the cabin logs. After having tried several types of notches on the outhouse we found this locking notch, which required no nails, to be the best for our needs. I rough-cut each corner with the chainsaw, then Sally carefully carved out the notches with a hammer and a chisel. After the corner notches were completed, we rolled the first log over. It fell into place with a satisfying thud, fitting tightly to the base log.

Our second log was not as successful—I had miscalculated the depth of the notch, and it fit poorly. Because we had spent half a day measuring and cutting the notches, this misfit was terribly disappointing. I rolled the log from the cabin in disgust, and vowed that our home would not be just a rough-hewn shelter with corners chopped out by axe—we wanted each notch to be perfect, each log to fit just right.

It took another full day to complete the first round of logs, but the result of our careful measuring and chiselling was a round of logs that nestled snugly against the base logs and notches that fitted so tightly we had to drive some together with the sledge hammer.

Completion of the floor and first round of the cabin was a reason for celebration. We held what I called a "round-up" party with a bush-style meal made with freeze-dried chili, brown rice, and dried green beans. Powdered orange juice and dried fruit completed our simple meal. We roasted the last of our marshmallows over an open fire as a special treat. It began to rain, but this didn't deter us. We donned our rain gear and continued the party.

Raising a metal cup, Sally made a toast to the start of our new home. Then we danced in the pouring rain on the newly completed cabin floor. In the city the sight of two people wearing yellow rubber rainsuits, dancing and singing in the rain, would be cause for concern. But in a remote forest with only moose and other wild animals watching us, we were uninhibited, and continued our rambunctious party until late in the evening.

During the long days which followed we worked steadily on the cabin, but our labours were frequently interrupted by visits from our bird and animal neighbours, who came to inspect our handiwork. It was hard to concentrate fully on cabin building while furtive weasels darted through the bush, squirrels chattered their comments from nearby trees, and chickadees perched on axe handles. Cheeky Canada jays swooped down to steal crumbs from our plates, and rusty blackbirds argued noisily amongst themselves. We felt like two workers with a legion of vociferous foremen.

Work on the cabin was halted abruptly one afternoon by Sally's call of, "Moose at the lake!" I dropped my tools and rushed towards the beach where a mother moose and her calf were browsing on willow bushes. Their long ears twitched ceaselessly to keep hungry mosquitoes away, but at the other end their short stubby tails were of little help. I was able to take many photographs before our subjects splashed into the lake and began to swim away.

"Quick, into the canoe," I whispered to Sally.

We jumped into the canoe to try for a picture of them in

the lake. All I could see of the large moose was a huge hairy snout and two long ears moving across the water. The calf followed close behind with its small brown nose held high above the surface and its spindly legs working furiously to keep up with its mother. Although Sally and I paddled at full speed, we didn't catch up to the moose until they reached the opposite shore. The massive cow shook herself, flinging droplets of water into the air, then casually looked at us over her shoulder and nudged the calf into the bushes.

Another visitor around camp was a prickly porcupine. As I was trimming a difficult notch one evening, I reached over the cabin wall to pick up an axe and startled the chubby creature. It had been nibbling contentedly on the axe handle. The porcupine thrashed his bristling tail, donating some quills to my glove and the cabin wall, then grunted and slowly waddled away. I was fortunate to be wearing gloves—a handful of quills from this mobile pincushion would have been very painful. I had read that salty axe handles were a favourite snack of porcupines, so from that day on we were careful to keep tools out of their reach.

"Porky" became a regular visitor around camp. The next day we found him trying to climb the food cache, but the aluminum around the tops of the poles effectively stopped him. When he waddled through camp his fat body jiggled and his hair and quills quivered with every clumsy step. He was a peaceful, slow-moving fellow, and although a porcupine is not an animal I would choose as a pet, we grew quite fond of our amusing companion.

Hordes of hungry mosquitoes were another constant distraction while we worked on the cabin. We thought the rain would keep them away. It didn't. We hoped the wind would drive them off. It couldn't. On the few sunny days, we expected the heat to keep them in the swamps. No chance. With only two humans per billion bugs, our blood was in constant demand. The buzzing, biting beasts were *everywhere*, and our only escape was in the tent, from where we heard the drone of millions of mosquitoes buzzing just outside the door.

Northern woodsmen of pioneer days had used a foul mixture of bear fat, pine tar and citronella, which no doubt kept more than just the mosquitoes away. We used liberal coat-

Trimming floorboards

Chiselling a notch

Another day, another log!

ings of bottled insect repellant. We also wore mosquito headnets—a brimmed hat with fine mesh netting which surrounds the head and closes around the neck with an elastic. Unfortunately a mosquito would sometimes manage to get in as I put my headnet on, and buzz around inside, driving me almost crazy.

Despite all the distractions, we were able to notch and place a complete round of logs most days. Progress often seemed slow, but we knew that a well-constructed cabin would make the difference between a comfortable and a cold winter. Whenever we were tempted to rush a notch I remembered another northern proverb the old trapper had repeated for us, "In this country you can spend time in the summer buildin' a tight cabin, or time freezin' your fingers choppin' wood in the winter to heat a drafty one!"

We took turns collecting buckets of moss from the forest floor, then used it to fill any gaps between the logs and corner notches. Sally designed and whittled a blunt tool, perfect for packing the moss tightly between the logs. Early settlers had chinked their cabins with everything from mud to manure, but spaghnum moss was our first choice for insulation.

As we worked on the cabin I gained a new insight into Sally's strengths and skills. Although Sally was not physically as strong as I, she tackled every task I did. Our wilderness home was a shared dream and a shared project, from hauling logs to sawing notches. At first I had insisted on doing most of the chainsaw work myself, but soon Sally asserted, "Hey, it's my cabin too—there's no reason why I can't take a turn cutting notches!"

We worked well together. It took patience to recarve a notch after rolling a heavy log into place and finding it didn't fit just right, and it took a certain sense of humour to laugh after hitting a badly bruised thumb with a hammer for the third time in an hour. During the few weeks we had been at Hottah Lake we had shared many trials and triumphs of outdoor life. These experiences and our mutual love of nature brought Sally and me closer together than our hectic city lives would have allowed. By working as a team, we saw our dream slowly come true.

It seemed as though we slipped into the past as wood

chips and shavings piled up around our feet. We shared the same satisfaction the pioneers must have experienced in hearing the dull thump of each log as corner notches dropped into place, and felt a strong sense of pride as the walls of our log cabin grew higher. Each notch was our own; each log was cut, peeled, and placed by our own hands.

But after four rounds of wall logs we found it impossible to heave the three-hundred-pound timbers into place. I considered several possibilities, including constructing a ramp of logs, then finally decided to hang a winch from a tripod built of poles. We cut three long, sturdy poles, tied them together at the top with nylon rope, and then placed the tripod at one corner of the cabin.

Our first plan was to use a shiny new contraption we had brought, which was billed as "the amazing pocket block and tackle," to lift the heavy logs. The colourful label claimed the gadget was capable of lifting one ton. A leaflet showed illustrations of people pulling cars out of ditches, lifting moose by the antlers, and other herculean feats—obviously drawn by an artist with a vivid imagination.

I untangled miles of thin nylon cord from seven plastic pulleys, then suspended the block and tackle from the tripod. After hooking the apparatus to one end of a log, we pulled with all our combined strength on the thin cord. The log didn't even budge! Not one inch. It appeared that the seven pulleys and all the cord created too much friction. I felt foolish for being so gullible.

"Oh well, the cord will make a great clothesline," Sally consoled me.

In the end, we hung our rusty, but trusty, come-along from the tripod and hooked it up to one end of the log.

"Pull! . . . Pull!..." Slowly, we winched the heavy log up. Each pull on the come-along lifted the log up only six inches, and it took us almost twenty minutes to lift one end into place.

"Sure glad this is going to be a low cabin!" Sally remarked as we wrestled the awkward tripod to the other end, and began winching.

"Watch out!" Sally yelled as the top end of the log slid off the cabin and crashed to the ground. Although I had nailed a block of wood onto the log, it had not held the log in place.

Lifting a heavy log

Cutting a window

The cabin from inside

"That was a little too close!" I shuddered. Sally and I had been very careful to avoid potential accidents. We always wore gloves, safety goggles, and steel-toed boots while working on the cabin. In fact, we were almost paranoid about safety. Even though we both had extensive first aid skills, our limited medical supplies and remote location could have turned even a moderately serious injury into a life or death situation.

Slowly, carefully, we winched the log back up onto the cabin, standing a respectable distance back in case the rope broke or the log slipped. I then wrapped a chain around the log to hold it in place, and winched the other end up without incident. It had taken us almost an hour to lift the log up to the cabin wall.

"It's backwards!" I said, then broke into laughter as Sally spun around to look at the log we had just raised. That was one mistake we hadn't made, but the look of horror on Sally's face was well worth the joke.

As the walls grew higher, each round of logs took longer to complete. It not only took longer to lift the logs up, but it was also more difficult and time-consuming to carve notches while balancing on a wall log six feet off the ground.

Finally, in early August, we heaved the last wall log into place. It took a day to cut openings for the door and three windows. We spent another full day with a hammer and chisel carefully finishing the window frames, then fitting the Plexiglass windows. At last, our small cabin was beginning to look like a home.

Five weeks of exhausting work had passed since we cut down the first tree for the cabin; we were bone-weary but felt a contentment that came with seeing our dream cabin slowly take shape.

Sally and I stood by the cabin, each holding a mug of tea in tired hands. I reached an arm around Sally's shoulders and pulled her close.

"We're getting there," I said quietly. "Just like the old-timer said—one log at a time."

CHAPTER 8

Home in the Woods

Visitors of the two-legged variety were few at our camp. Sally and I had not seen another person for almost six weeks, and when a plane we didn't recognize flew low over the lake in early August, we did what anyone in our situation would do—we stampeded to the lake.

We waved frantically from the beach. Our excitement mounted as we watched the small floatplane descend towards the water.

"Quick! Let's get the canoe," Sally yelled. "We can paddle out to meet it!"

"Hold on a minute," I called to her as I raced to the tent. Once inside, I ransacked the boxes and bags, looking for an envelope and paper. Finally, after emptying our belongings all over the bed and strewing paper on the floor, I found them. I dashed back to the lakeshore, where Sally was already in the canoe, waiting impatiently.

"I brought writing paper," I explained hastily.

I jumped into the canoe, grabbed a paddle, then remembered something of importance.

"Oh no . . . a pen!" I shouted. I leapt into knee deep water and ran up the beach. By the time I'd found the pen and dashed back the second time, I was out of breath.

"You paddle like mad," I managed to say between breaths. "I'll write a quick letter to Mom and Dad so we can give it to the pilot!"

The plane had already cut into the lake's smooth surface and was taxiing towards the sandy point across the lake. As Sally paddled, I quickly scribbled a hello and news of the last months.

"Tell them about . . . the moose that swam . . . by our canoe last week . . . and the fishing . . . and the mosquitoes!" Sally was a little out of breath from paddling hard and fast.

Even though I was having a tough time writing because the canoe bobbed and surged with Sally's every paddle stroke, I took a moment between pen strokes to encourage her to paddle faster. But we were only halfway across the lake when she slowed down noticeably.

"I can't keep paddling by myself," Sally groaned. "Write the letter when we get there!"

I'm not sure what the visitors thought when they saw two crazed individuals paddling furiously towards them. We hadn't taken time to change from grubby work clothes, and must have looked like wild bushmen. Sally was colourfully garbed in a torn wool shirt, a tattered pair of sapstained jeans, and wore a red bandanna around her head. My own appearance was even more bizarre, accented by a head-to-toe coating of woodchips and sawdust. An axe, left in the canoe from a previous outing, rested at my feet, completing our savage guise.

If they were frightened, it didn't show. A smiling, rotund man in hip waders pulled the canoe ashore, and held out a chocolate bar as a peace offering.

"Hi," he said. "We saw your camp as we flew by. I kinda thought you might paddle over for a visit."

It turned out that our visitors were three sport fishermen on a lake-to-lake fishing trip in northern B.C.

"Didn't think anything lived in this country but moose and mosquitoes!" the pilot said. "How's the fishing?"

"Great fishing—the rainbow trout are delicious," I assured him.

Sally and I babbled like two excited children, telling

stories about our wilderness life and animal neighbours. The largest fisherman listened earnestly as Sally talked about our limited provisions, then reached into his fishing creel and handed her a small paper bag.

"I think you'll need these more than me," he winked. Sally peeped into the bag, and her eyes widened with delight.

"Four chocolate bars!"

I quizzed the pilot for information about the surrounding area. "Seen any wildlife? Does the Tucho valley look marshy? What does the valley to the west look like?"

"Well, there looks to be a beautiful little lake over that way," he said, pointing westward, "and we saw a high open valley just north of your lake. We even spotted a herd of caribou there."

Sally and I talked with the fishermen for almost an hour, then finally left them to catch trout in peace.

We could hardly wait to have time to go hiking and try to photograph the caribou that the pilot had mentioned. The next morning we returned to work on the cabin with renewed energy. We tackled the difficult project of building the upper front and rear walls, called gables, which would support the roof beams.

It took two days to raise the logs, nail them in place, and cut the tricky triangular gables to the correct angle. Then came the most difficult part of building the cabin—lifting the heavy roof support beams onto the finished gables. It took teamwork and all of our combined strength to lift the four-hundred-pound logs using only the small come-along, muscle, and sweat. The ridge pole was the most difficult; we slowly hoisted the hefty beam up to the top wall log, then pulled and rolled the log up the incline of the roof to the peak.

At this point the cabin looked complete from the front, but, like a storefront in a western movie, it lacked a roof. We planned to build the roof with small poles, but finding two hundred straight poles that were ten feet long, three inches in diameter and without too much taper proved to be a real challenge. I think we found a total of two that met those specifications.

Our standards dropped as the monotonous project continued. "This one is only two and a half inches," Sally said with as she measured the base of a scrawny looking tree.

"O.K." I replied.

"Four inches?" Sally asked.

"Well . . . O.K." All trees were worth consideration. We needed too many poles for the roof to be fussy.

"This one has a bit of a curve," Sally called.

"Cut it down!"

Peeling bark off the two hundred poles was a long procedure, but necessary unless we were willing to put up with bark beetles moving in and showering us with sawdust through the winter. We nailed the peeled poles side by side on top of the roof support beams. Next, we gathered bucketloads of moss to fill the spaces between the poles, so the cabin would be well insulated.

"Let's get that roof on before we get snowed-in!" I said one morning. I was not speaking entirely in jest. Although it was only mid-August, there was new snow on the mountains—a real incentive for us to speed up our cabin-building efforts.

While Sally finished packing moss between the roof poles, I cut a hole for the stove pipe. A small metal shield and support would hold the pipe in place. Finally, we nailed roofing paper over the poles and moss. Roofing paper was one of the few concessions we made to man-made materials—we wanted a leakproof roof!

Our calculations for roofing paper and nails left no room for error; because of the space and weight limitations of the floatplane which brought our gear in, we had packed only three rolls of tarpaper and just enough nails to complete the job. By the time we finished the roof, there was only a twelve-inch square of tarpaper and a handful of nails left.

The final touch in making the log cabin a home was to build a front door. We crafted our front door by cutting three logs in half lengthwise and carefully fitting them together. To hold the door together we nailed a Z shaped cross-brace of small logs on the outside.

"No bear is going to bust this down," I said as we dragged the heavy door to the cabin. After trimming it to fit the opening, we mounted two large hinges on the frame. Then we manoeuvred the "two-ton" door into place. I

A gable end

Finishing touches

Working on the roof

shimmed the bottom with small scraps of wood, and installed each hinge with only one lag screw to see how the door would pivot.

I beamed with surprise as the door swung open easily without need for any further adjustment.

A handle fashioned from a deer antler added a certain touch of elegance. I had also found a large pair of moose antlers in the forest and insisted that our cabin would not be complete until we hung the antlers on the front wall. Once I had nailed the antlers into place above the front door, we stepped back to view our small log cabin.

"Looks like we knew what we were doing, after all," Sally said, looking appraisingly at our handiwork.

The log cabin was a dream come true for us—one that we had often feared would never come true during the hard days of felling, peeling and hauling logs, and of lifting and notching massive timbers. After two months of hard work, we finally had a home in the woods.

"Look," I said. A mischievous pine marten had already come by and claimed the moose antlers above the front door as a comfortable resting spot. We were pleased that our cabin was beginning to be accepted by the animals as part of the forest.

The first step in moving into our new home was to install our small woodburning stove in the centre of the cabin. We dragged the heavy stove across the threshold, then placed it on top of a large sheet of aluminum designed to keep sparks from landing on the wood floor.

That evening, we celebrated the completion of our new home with an old-fashioned house-warming party. As the stove warmed the cabin, drying the logs and the moss insulation, we enjoyed a festive evening with spruce needle tea, blueberry bannock, and our own banjo and fiddle music. The small cabin and warm stove were luxury after months in the cold, damp tent. We would sleep by an upright wall which didn't flap in the wind and under a roof that was more substantial than a thin layer of canvas. And the room! Compared with our tent, the sixteen-by-eighteen-foot cabin seemed like a mansion.

As we sat by the woodburning stove, I thought of the work we had put into building the cabin, and how it had changed us. We had become more self-confident, more aware of our strengths and weaknesses. It wasn't simply that we had worked hard and had learned how to carve a home from the wilderness; we had learned a great deal about ourselves and about each other. And by working as a team, we had grown closer.

By leaving our protective city environment for this rugged, challenging life, we had also learned to live with risk. We knew that either one of us could at any moment be crushed under a falling tree, or possibly be attacked by a wild animal. This knowledge affected our sense of life in a profound way. Perhaps this was why we had come to the north—to test ourselves and discover our limits in an environment which would hold us accountable for our every action. Our remote existence and dangers of the wild also made life seem more real, and precious.

Thinking of these things, we edged closer to the reassuring warmth of the woodburning stove. As the yellow, mellow glow of our kerosene lantern lit the cabin, we felt a warmth not only from the fire, but also from the satisfaction of watching the amber firelight flicker against the walls of the home we had built together.

We spent the following days making our new home more comfortable. A bed was my first priority—after sleeping on the cold, hard ground for more than two months, I wanted a comfortable bed more than any other piece of furniture! In the left rear corner of the cabin we built a frame of heavy poles, supported by bed posts of peeled spruce. Because our cabin had so little floor space, we made the bed high enough to allow boxes to be stored underneath the bed.

I had thought out my design carefully: we would be supported by a heavy plastic tarp, with grommets spaced six inches apart around the edge. The tarp would be tied to the bed frame with strong nylon rope laced through the grommets.

"How could that tarp possibly hold our weight?" Sally asked. She felt our weight would tear the grommets out of the plastic. I was sure my design would work.

"You obviously don't understand the *physics* of this," I chided. I reasoned that since our combined weight was less than three hundred pounds and there were thirty-six grommets, there would be less than ten pounds stress per grommet.

After stringing the tarp I graciously offered Sally the first try on the luxurious bed, but for some reason she declined. I lay on the well-engineered structure and closed my eyes contentedly.

"Ahh, bliss," I sighed—then heard a strange ripping noise. Without further warning the grommets tore out of the side of the tarp I lay on, and I was rudely dropped onto the floor.

"So much for physics!" Sally laughed as I picked up my bruised body and ego.

The new, improved, design—engineered by Sally—was a criss-cross grid of nylon ropes spaced three inches apart. On top of this we placed our foam mattress and sleeping bags. We later found that the only problem with this design was that nylon rope stretches. We had to tighten our bed every two weeks.

Other hand-made furniture included a table made of split logs, and two stumps for chairs. We built a low counter along the front wall to serve as a writing desk, hoping that the view of the lake through the front window would inspire us. The desk continued along the west wall, and above the desk we built bookshelves of poles. On a shelf near the bed we placed a prospector's gold pan to be used as a wash basin, and on the wall we tacked a piece of aluminum foil as a mirror and a deer antler as a towel rack.

"I'd like the kithen counter here, at just the right height for baking," Sally said, drawing a line along the east wall.

"Great, why don't you build it yourself—to your specifications," I suggested.

"I think I will. Yours would probably collapse," Sally teased.

Sally designed and constructed a long, sturdy counter of poles. My contribution was a three-foot section of aluminum to provide a smooth surface for kneading bread, and a row of nails along the wall to hang the cast-iron pots and pans.

An assortment of metal containers kept our food away from small rodents. Our pet mouse had already moved into the cabin, but we decided that as long as he didn't invite any friends or relatives we would let him stay. We enjoyed his

A house-warming party!

Inside the cabin

company and allowed that he would be a great cabin vacuum cleaner, cleaning up any crumbs from the floor.

Our small cabin may not have won any "design of the year" awards, but it was warm and snug. The interior decor of the cabin could best be described as Early Canadian Rustic, in muted wood tones with the inlaid green moss between each log providing a complementary colour. Handhewn pine furnishings completed the rustic theme, more from available materials than a devotion to interior decoration. A home seems more cozy with plants, and ours included grass and fireweed growing up between the floorboards and moss hanging down between the roof poles.

Each window framed a picture more attractive than any painted on canvas. On each side of our log wall gallery was a landscape portrait of pine trees and auburn willows set against an azure sky. The front window looked out on a scene of tall, dark mountains, green forest, and an emerald lake. In the foreground a narrow, curving path wound through long tawny grass to a sandy beach. It was through these windows that we would watch the changing seasons and scenery for the next year.

Until colder weather came, I devised a way to hold the Plexiglass windows in place with removable nails. Because mosquito season was almost over, we enjoyed removing the windows so that we could listen to the wind whispering in the treetops and to animals rustling through the forest outside our cabin. Even when we were inside the cabin, we could be part of the busy world outside; from our bed we heard sparrows and chickadees singing, and one morning a small hummingbird flew in the door, buzzed around the cabin, then departed out the east window.

We were also enchanted by the pleasant gurgling of the creek wending its way down the mountainside, sounding near, then far away, at the whim of the wind. In the ever-changing sounds of falling water we could hear the music of the north country—a symphony of imaginary sounds, from the deep, resonant oboe to the rapid thumping of a timpani or trilling of a flute. Sometimes when the wind changed we heard a soft melody, almost like the strains of harp music.

Noisy neighbours were a bit of a problem, though. On our second morning in the cabin we were rudely wakened from a restful sleep. CRASH! BANG! THUMP! Whatever animal was out there sounded mean and ferocious. I immediately assumed that a bear was prowling around the cabin.

"Get the gun, Sally!" I whispered hoarsely.

"Get it yourself," she replied, pushing me out of the sleeping bag.

The loud crashing continued as I nervously crawled out of bed, tiptoed to the window, then peered out—right into the wicked green eyes of the intruder. Our eyes met for a long moment.

"What is it?" Sally asked nervously.

As my eyes adjusted to the dim light, I saw the beast. It was only a small marten. The marten bounded along the woodpile, knocking more pieces of wood against the cabin wall, then scampered away.

When our heartbeats had returned to normal we laughed at our fears, feeling foolish that we had entertained visions of vicious beasts. Fortunately, instances of wild animals attacking humans are far less common than folk-lore suggests—but knowing this had provided us with little comfort when we first heard the noises.

Sally and I were awakened only an hour later by a loud scratching and scuffing on the roof of the cabin. We crept outside with a lantern to find out who our noisy visitor was this time, and saw a small face peering over the edge of the roof.

"It's a weasel!" I laughed. The weasel was mesmerized by the glow of the lantern for a minute, then scrambled up to the peak of the roof and slid down the other side.

"If this is the kind of excitement that comes with cabin living, we should have quite a year!" Sally commented.

CHAPTER 9

Indian Summer

With the cabin completed, Sally and I finally had time to relax—we sat on the doorstep, basking in the sun and watching a squirrel scamper up and down a pine tree.

"Do you know what the date is?" Sally asked absently.

"Dunno, last time I marked off the calendar was August twenty-third."

"Aren't Jim and Vern coming to visit on the twenty-eighth?" she questioned.

We had been looking forward to our friends' visit all summer but somehow, in the excitement of moving into the cabin, we had lost track of the date. Now we scanned the calendar anxiously—according to the X's, Jim and Vern would arrive with our next supply flight in one or two days.

Suddenly, our lazy morning was transformed into a flurry of activity. We dragged away the last debris from log cutting, swept the cabin floor clear of bits moss and sawdust, and cut extra stools from rounds of wood. Once the cabin seemed reasonably neat we did a huge laundry and prepared the tent for our visitors. Then Sally insisted that I tidy myself up for our guests.

"Time for a shave and a haircut," Sally said, eyeing my scraggly beard and unkempt hair critically. She armed herself with a pair of bandage scissors and prepared to make her debut as a barber.

"Watch out for the ears!" I cautioned her nervously as I sat on a stump.

"Don't worry—I'll only trim off half an inch," my barber said. *Snip, snip, snip.*

After a few minutes of confident scissor-work Sally stood back and surveyed my hair for a moment, then smiled and mumbled something inaudible.

"What was that?" I asked, my voice a bit strained.

"Oh, nothing much. I just noticed the left side is a bit shorter than the right. Guess I'll have to take off an inch, after all." *Snip, snip.*

When the job was finished, Sally assured me that it looked "just great!" I had to take her word for it as the mirror on the compass was too small to reveal much. I picked up the scissors and studied Sally's hair.

"I think I'll grow mine long," she said quickly, ending my thoughts of retaliation.

The next day, we began a baking spree, making bread, biscuits, dozens of cookies, and bran muffins filled with wild crowberries. Sally also wanted a cake for the occasion. The recipe book made baking a cake look so easy, but our first difficulty was in selecting a recipe for which we had the ingredients.

"This is so frustrating," Sally said. "How am I supposed to make a cake when so many recipes call for whipping cream, bananas, or fresh eggs?"

"Try the Northern Cookbook," I suggested. "Betty Crocker has probably never been out of an air-conditioned kitchen!"

But even the Northern Cookbook gave us some trouble; after we found a suitable recipe, the first simple instruction was, "Heat oven to 350 degrees." It took us half an hour to cut an adequate stack of dry firewood, get the fire going, and set up the folding oven on the woodburning stove.

Once the fire was ready, Sally picked up the cookbook and read out loud, "Lightly grease an eight-inch cake pan with butter. . . . "

"Uh, two problems," I laughed. "No butter, and no eight-inch cake tin. Why did you bring a book like that?"

We decided two bread pans would work almost as well as a cake tin and that vegetable oil would do to grease the pans. We had to improvise a little over the ingredients, too, substituting reconstituted powdered eggs and milk for the fresh variety called for in the recipe. Although we didn't have butter, we did have a precious supply of margarine which we stored in a five-gallon bucket in the lake.

Then (oh, the words made it sound so simple), "Blend for three minutes at high speed." The batter was so thick that our tiny eggbeater wouldn't even turn! Sally sat on the floor with the bowl gripped between her knees and stirred vigorously with a wooden spoon for six arduous minutes, then finally slid the cakes into the tiny oven. We nursed the fire to maintain the right heat and kept a close eye on the oven's thermometer. An hour later we peeked in to see what the result was.

"Wow, they look like real cakes!" I exclaimed. Even with all the deviations from the recipe, the cakes looked as light and fluffy as any baked in an electric oven.

"I think that I should taste-test everything before Jim and Vern come," I suggested, reaching for one of the pans.

"You can wait until they get here to sample the goodies!" Sally replied firmly.

"Well, O.K. I guess that's tomorrow . . . I can wait that long."

"You know, I'm kind of nervous about their visit," I confided to Sally later. "Do you think we'll be tongue-tied?"

"You mean, are we *bushed*?" Sally asked. "Probably. It's been a long time since we talked with anyone else." Although we looked forward to Jim and Vern's visit, we were a little apprehensive about suddenly sharing our world after having been alone for so long.

Sally and I slept fitfully that night and were up at dawn the next morning. Tense and excited, we waited at the beach. Would Jim and Vern be able to visit us after all? Was this the right day? Was the weather fair enough for flying?

All morning long we paced back and forth between the cabin and the waterfront, straining to hear any distant sound that might be a plane. Finally, around noon, the drone of the Beaver floatplane reverberated through the valley. The yellow-and-blue plane roared low over the cabin, then splashed onto the lake, giving our visitors a bumpy initiation to northern life.

Jim and Vern had hardly stepped off the plane when we let fly a hurricane of questions. "How was the drive up? How was the flight? Did you manage to fit all of our supplies into the plane? Have you got your hiking boots?" They laughed at our excitement and gave Sally a couple of warm hugs.

While we unloaded the plane, we learned that their flight had been as much a white-knuckle experience as ours had been.

"You should have seen Vern's eyes bug out when his door flew open in midair!" Jim laughed.

"All Beavers are built like that," Jeff, the pilot, assured us. "Important parts like the prop are held on pretty good, though!"

The plane was packed like a bulging suitcase. When we asked Jeff if he'd had any problems with the load he answered calmly, "It was kinda heavy—I've never seen the floats so low in the water before."

The cargo included boxes of food, bulky winter clothes, and a large carton crammed with letters, parcels, and other goodies. Jim lifted a second overstuffed carton out of the plane and invited us to open it. He had thoughtfully packed foods he knew we would be craving—homemade pickles and jam, fresh vegetables, steaks, bacon, four dozen unbroken eggs, and many other treats. No wonder Jeff felt the plane was overloaded!

"Let's see the cabin, then canoe around the lake, then do some hiking!" Jim urged, as enthusiastic as we had been when we first arrived at the lake.

Proudly, we showed them around the cabin, and beamed while they ran their hands admiringly over the tightly-fit wall logs. I pointed out each difficult log, the door, and our hand-hewn furniture. We finished with a tour of the camp, highlighting the airy outhouse and twelve-foot-high food cache.

"See those strips of aluminum around the poles?" I said. "They're to prevent hungry animals like porcupines or wolverines from climbing the poles and eating our food."

"A good precaution," Vern said. "But I'm afraid nothing as simple as that will keep Jim out!" I chuckled. Jim was famous for his appetite.

"Speaking of food . . . ," Jim hinted, rubbing his stomach. At Jim's insistence, we headed back to the cabin for a special lunch that Sally and I had prepared—fresh bread, baked beans, and blueberry muffins.

After lunch, we took Jim and Vern on a canoe trip to the east end of Hottah Lake. The phrase, "don't rock the boat," took on a new meaning with four people in the canoe. Each time one of our guests shifted his weight, the canoe tipped wildly from one side to the other. I could tell by Sally's erratic paddle strokes that she was nervous, and when Vern asked if he could try fishing, I had some reservations. I figured that if Vern, who was six feet tall, so much as stretched out an arm to cast a lure, the canoe would surely tip.

At first there were no problems. . . . Then Vern hooked into a rainbow trout.

"Way to go!" Jim cheered. "I'll net the fish for you."

Neither of our guests seemed to have any fear of being capsized. Sally and I looked at each other apprehensively, but held our tongues until Jim, chasing the leaping trout with the net, leaned over the edge of the canoe.

"You'll tip the boat!" Sally yelled as we both leaned frantically in the other direction, trying to counterbalance Jim's weight.

"I've got it!" Jim called triumphantly as he hoisted the thrashing trout into the canoe and dropped it proudly at Sally's feet.

We had hardly recovered from the excitement of the first catch when Vern hooked another. The same pandemonium followed as we desperately tried to keep the canoe upright. Finally, after netting four trout and being reminded, "You catch 'em, you clean 'em," Vern decided that we had enough fish for a good feast.

Although Sally and I were accustomed to quiet canoe trips, this time we talked, told jokes, and bantered back and forth. I enthusiastically pointed out landmarks, and eagerly told stories of our wildlife encounters—there was so much to share.

"Could you paddle a little faster and talk a little slower?" Vern quipped after half an hour of non-stop chatter.

Then Sally motioned us to be quiet. "There's a beaver ahead," she whispered. We watched silently as it shuffled onto the shore and began chewing at a willow branch. Black fur glistened in the sunlight as the beaver waddled back to the water with the willow branch dangling from its mouth. Then, one of our paddles clunked against the canoe and the beaver dived under the water with a splash of its tail.

We continued down the lake, each one of us silent as we scanned the shoreline and lake for more animals or birds. Jim and Vern paddled while, for a change, Sally and I relaxed in the middle of the canoe.

"I'm glad we have company," Sally whispered. "This is as exciting as when we saw our lake for the first time, but it seems even more special sharing it with Jim and Vern."

At the end of Hottah Lake, we stopped for an early supper. Jim and I built a crackling campfire and pan fried the trout, while Sally showed Vern how to prepare bannock. As we ate, we all gazed at the sparkling lake, and the rugged peaks surrounding us.

"This is the life," Vern sighed. "I envy you two, spending a whole year here."

My thoughts flashed back to Vern's reaction when I had first told him we were going to Hottah Lake. He had asked why we wanted to spend so long in the wilderness. I felt that he now understood.

By the time we arrived back at the cabin, the sun was setting behind distant peaks. We talked until late evening, when Jim and Vern retired to their tent, exhausted. Sally and I stayed up to read our mail by candlelight. Comments in the letters ranged from, "I shouldn't tell you this, but we had our first local corn yesterday," to "I sometimes wish I was up there with you... until I think about the mosquitoes!" Finally, when we could hardly keep our eyes open, we went to bed.

Jim was first into the cabin the next morning and was full of energy. "How about climbing that peak behind your cabin?" he suggested.

Although Sally and I were familiar with the route, our pace was slow as we made frequent stops to sample wild blueberries and crowberries in the forest. Vern was particularly appreciative of the interruptions because he was breaking in a new pair of boots. Or, as he grimaced, "They're breaking me in!"

After three hours, we emerged from the protection of the forest and were hit by gusts of cold wind which swept across the open alpine slope. We found shelter behind a large boulder and viewed the stormy landscape below us. Dark clouds scudded along the mountain tops and we could feel the raw power of the approaching storm in the hollow howling of the wind, which snatched words from our mouths as we spoke.

Vern balked when I suggested continuing to the summit. "This is far enough for me," he said firmly, zipping up the hood of his parka.

We left Vern to rest at the treeline, then slowly trudged upward, buffeted by gusts of wind which flattened the grass and bent small trees with its fury. The sight of rapidly approaching storm clouds made us turn back only five hundred feet from the summit—we decided the open slope would have been a poor place to be caught in a thunderstorm.

When we returned to the protection of the trees we found Vern bundled up in a space blanket, and fast asleep. Jim and I quietly discussed devious ways of rousing him.

"Tie his shoelaces together and yell BEAR!" Jim suggested. But before I could come up with a nastier idea, Vern awoke, thwarting our plans.

We headed down the mountain, and arrived at camp just as it started to rain. I thought Jim and Vern would have wanted to sit out the storm inside the cabin, but they were eager to stay outdoors and were well equipped with rain gear.

"I can sit inside when I'm in Vancouver," Jim explained. "I came here to rough it for a week. What can we help with?"

One project we needed assistance with was raising a thirty-foot pole for our radio antenna. We had tried the radio through the summer, but had not been able to reach anyone. I felt that if we could mount the antenna high enough, the radio might transmit better.

We found a dry pole to use as a mast, then attached the antenna with clamps and fastened three guy wires to the pole. It took all four of us to raise the awkward, forty-foot structure into place beside the cabin. Then I tried the radio. The crackling and static had definitely increased in volume, but we would have to wait for better weather to hear any other radio operators.

Jim and Vern's energy and enthusiasm for outdoor life matched ours. Although we had been worried about how to entertain our friends for a week, our concerns were unfounded—they were both seasoned campers and enjoyed the outdoors. However, they had never been so far removed from civilization and were very intrigued with our rustic lifestyle. Carrying water from the lake, splitting wood, and tending the fire were all tasks which our guests gladly shared.

Sally and I especially enjoyed the times when we could pair off with Jim or Vern and talk with someone other than each other. Each day was an opportunity to share our thoughts and our way of life with friends, and through the week we discussed everything from politics to porcupines.

"Do you think you'll ever go back to your job?" Jim asked suddenly, as we were deep in a discussion about lifestyles.

I paused for a long moment, then answered quietly, "I don't think so." Sally and I had only been in the wilderness for two and a half months, but hearing news from the "outside" world gave me a new perspective on our life. It did not inspire me to ever want to leave the wilderness.

The last two days with our guests brought clear, Indian summer weather. We canoed around the lake and explored along the Tucho River, wanting to share as much of our wilderness as we could.

On the evening before they were to leave, Jim and Vern went on a final fishing trip while Sally and I completed long letters to friends, possibly the last we would mail until next summer.

The morning of September fourth, the day that Jim and Vern were to be picked up, brought a sudden change in the weather. Nearby mountain peaks were dusted with new snow and the shrubs around the cabin were fringed with frost. It seemed that summer was finally over.

"It looks as if you might be snowed-in for the winter. Maybe we should start building you a cabin," I joked. The expression on Jim's face showed he wouldn't have minded that at all.

We heard the drumming of the Beaver floatplane just after noon, and rushed down to the beach to watch the plane land. The pilot beached the aircraft, then we watched him emerge from the cockpit with an armload of vegetables, fresh from his garden—a real treat for us, and a show of true northern hospitality.

"I couldn't squeeze all of your food boxes into the plane," Jeff said apologetically, "but Ron or I will bring them by in late October before the lake freezes."

Jim and Vern gave us amused glances as we unloaded an odd assortment of boxes, as well as snowshoes, and six pairs of skis.

"In case you're wondering about the skis, we each have one pair of mountaineering, one pair of light touring, and one pair of no-wax skis," I explained.

"What, no water skis?" Vern scoffed.

Jim and Vern climbed reluctantly into the plane for their return to civilization. "You sure you don't want to trade places?" Jim teased as he fastened his seatbelt and rattled the loose door.

We waved goodbye as the floatplane roared down the lake, and stood watching until the plane became a speck in the distance.

That evening, Sally and I reminisced about highlights of the last week—our adventures, late night crib games, and the stories and jokes we had exchanged by the warm stove. It had been an action-packed week, but we were content to return to the routine of our quiet life. We looked forward to quiet winter evenings in our cozy log cabin, days spent exploring our untamed surroundings, and the challenge of living totally dependent upon our own resources.

CHAPTER 10

Autumn Days

Autumn was an exciting and colourful time in our northern valley. Rutting moose bashed through the forest and grunted loud calls to their mates, and brilliant northern lights danced in the night sky, signalling a change of seasons. Birch and willow trees, sensing colder weather, exchanged their cool green colours for the warm yellow, bronze and crimson hues of fall.

Our outdoor life was a world of new sights as brilliant pink fireweed decorated the forest and willow bushes around our cabin were dressed with golden leaves. The colours of autumn became more intense each day until the forest seemed almost to glow with the fiery hues.

Sally and I spent many pleasant autumn afternoons picking berries to dry for our winter food supply. Our wild harvest of red currants, blueberries, and crowberries provided a welcome change from dried fruit. But bear tracks near the berry patches indicated that we were not the only ones enjoying nature's harvest, and we would look over our shoulders every few minutes to make sure there were no bears approaching for a last snack before hibernation.

With the cabin finished and the growl of the chainsaw no longer breaking the silence, animals wandered more freely through our clearing. One morning I opened the front door to find a bull moose with large antlers almost on the door-step. The moose loudly snorted his surprise and stared at me for a moment, then turned and charged into the forest.

Many birds also visited the cabin, waking us each morning with a cheerful medley of songs. Chickadees had learned to come by each day for handouts sprinkled on the ground, and Canada jays squawked saucily from their perch in the antlers above the front door where we left granola. Many types of ducks and shorebirds floated in our bay as they rested on their way south for the winter.

One morning in early September I heard a faint, familiar, resonant sound from the north.

"Geese!" I called to Sally, then rushed to the lake to watch a flock of forty Canada geese winging through the sky in a large V-formation. The geese flew over the cabin, with their long, black necks outstretched and large wings undulating effortlessly. The musical, honking medley became louder as the flock circled, then descended into the mist at the east end of Hottah Lake.

The low morning fog shrouded the lake as we paddled towards our vocal visitors. Dark forms of twisted and leaning trees loomed along the shoreline, and the only sound on the hushed lake was the rhythmical dipping of our paddles. The geese were quiet now, and we guessed they had landed. Then, the forlorn wail of a loon echoed from somewhere in the fog, adding to the eerie effect.

By the time we reached the east end of Hottah Lake, the morning mist was thinning, revealing brilliant patches of blue sky. We paddled slowly along the shoreline, hoping to get close enough to photograph the geese.

The large birds were resting quietly where a creek entered the lake, but as we approached they began honking nervously. First one goose called out, then another, until the entire flock responded with a cacophony of two-syllable *haronks*. As Sally and I paddled closer, the wary birds pattered awkwardly across the lake, then flew up with a thunderous slapping of wings on water. The flock noisily circled overhead then landed a few hundred yards away, skidding across the water on outstretched feet.

"How about trying to canoe up the creek?" I suggested, when it became apparent that the geese were not willing to be photographed. This small creek at the southeast corner of Hottah Lake had intrigued me for some time, and although the topographic map described the creek as intermittent, we thought it might be navigable by canoe.

The first half-mile of travel up Intermittent Creek was easy paddling, but then the creek split into three narrow channels. We knew that the deepest channel would have the strongest current, and we watched for bent underwater plants which pointed the way like green streamers. The small stream alternated between being shallow and almost impassable, to being deep and swift, then shallow again.

"This must be the 'intermittent' part shown on the map," Sally said, shivering as we jumped barefoot into the cold water and heaved the canoe over another sand bar.

In spite of these obstacles, it was a scenic trip through the marshy lowland. Tufts of tall golden grass waved in the morning breeze, and red shoots of young willow growth sprouted from the weathered gray sticks and mud of an abandoned beaver lodge. The banks of the creek were decorated in the vivid bronze and gold hues of autumn foliage, as if splashed by an artist's brush.

The shoreline was dotted with small animal prints, which told stories of nocturnal wanderings. Muskrat tracks meandered along the water's edge, and another series of slender prints led to the creek, where a raccoon had paused to wash its supper. Farther along, we found a worn groove in the slippery bank where otters had slid into the water, and hundreds of footprints where they had run up for another turn. Looking at the tracks, we could visualize these playful animals loping up the slope again and again for the joy of sliding down.

The silty bottom of the creek was punctuated with moose tracks. The impressions were sharp and crisp-edged; the unsettled silt that still clouded the hollows hinted that the moose had been by only a short time before. The neatness of the tracks indicated that they had been made by a cow moose, not by a bull which would have dragged its feet.

We followed the creek as it wound through the wide

marsh and occasionally doubled back on itself; like a liquid maze, it led us to impassable channels. We struggled up the creek for a mile and a half, until the water became too shallow to canoe. Then we turned around and slowly drifted, paddled, and drifted with the current, enjoying the sights and sounds of the marsh.

Sally and I made our way down the creek in silence. Sound carries well over water, and talking would have decreased our chances of seeing or photographing wildlife. We had developed a harmonious teamwork, gained after canoeing together for many miles and many seasons. Sally usually paddled in the bow, and paused just long enough between each stroke for me to do a J-stroke, then our paddles re-entered the water in unison. "Change," spoken quietly, meant one more stroke, then we would change sides and continue without missing a beat.

"Mallards," I said softly as we rounded a bend. We watched the ducks upend to feed on underwater plants, leaving their orange feet comically paddling in the air. The males had striking satin-green heads, white neck rings and shiny brown chests, but the dull-brown females were hardly distinguishable from the surrounding marsh.

I slowly guided the canoe towards the ducks while Sally reached for the camera.

"Steady," Sally whispered as she focused the telephoto lense. We were able to take four photographs before the boisterous *quack, quack-quack* of a female warned the others of our approach. We stopped, and remained motionless until the ducks began feeding again. Slowly, quietly, I paddled forward.

Then it happened. . . . Sally took this fine opportunity to sneeze! The calm scene broke into a noisy pattering of feet and flapping of wings on water as the mallards took to the air, and went in search of a quieter pond.

"Good timing," I laughed. Sally looked annoyed at losing the opportunity to take more photographs.

Many other species of ducks rested in quiet backwaters of the creek. A mellow, whistling call lured us into a small pond where a pair of petite, green-winged teals dabbled in the reeds. Like many ducks, the male was the most colourful, with a cinnamon head and a glossy green mask around his eyes. Farther down the creek the distinctive whistling sound of goldeneyes echoed in the still air as they flew over the marsh.

As Sally and I canoed back across the lake, we discussed plans to do more exploring. Cabin-building during the summer had left little time to venture into new areas, and we were eager to make up for lost days. Mile after mile of unexplored country surrounded our cabin, but two small lakes to the northeast interested us the most.

We were up early the next morning, and were delighted to find another clear day. "That's a record—two nice days in a row," Sally grinned.

We began canoeing as the first rays of sunlight illuminated the valley with warm yellow light. As we entered the fjord-like inlet at the east end of Hottah Lake, we saw a family of loons. A young, mottled-brown loon popped up beside the canoe and began calling. Its call was like an adolescent boy's voice, breaking from tenor to soprano.

Sally cupped her hands over her mouth and called to the loons, mimicking their falsetto voices. *Whooeeoo*, a loon called back! The steep walls of the inlet echoed with a medley of loon calls, and with each echo another loon would answer, adding to the confusion. The loons must have felt they were surrounded by their kin, and for us, listening to the reverberating musical calls was like being in a concert hall of nature.

We continued up the inlet, then beached our canoe where a wild rushing river tumbled into the lake. A deeply-rutted moose path led up from the lake and wound through the trees along the left side of the river.

"Let's see if this trail leads to the next lake," I suggested.

After fifteen minutes of hiking we came to a thundering waterfall with frothy white water cascading over dark rocks. We were mesmerized by the sound and motion, and stood watching the wall of water for several minutes. Then we continued along the game path towards the next lake.

Suddenly, loud crashing and splashing noises came from the river. Our immediate reaction was to retreat, but as the grunting and crashing continued, our curiosity overcame our fear. We crept down the path, then watched as two moose clashed in an exciting but short-lived battle. The bulls collided in a fury of clunking antlers, thrashing hooves, and splashing water. The fight was over quickly. After two short rounds of battering antlers, the smaller moose was beaten and retreated into the forest.

The victor was an impressive-looking animal, with rippling muscles along his large shoulder hump, and white clouds of vapor issuing from flared nostrils. Normally, we might have stalked the moose to take photographs, but the usually docile animals were unpredictable and aggressive during autumn. This was rutting season; a time of challenges barked in the forest, and antlers clunking against antlers as the males competed in head-on battles to win a mate.

Then the bull moose abruptly turned towards us. The massive animal pawed the ground angrily and lowered his large antlers. He snorted loudly and pawed the ground again—then he slowly dropped his head to munch on a willow bush. We waited silently, until the moose had finished his breakfast and wandered away, before we cautiously resumed our hike.

The game path continued along the river bank to a small, pear-shaped lake nestled in a dark bowl of evergreen trees. Massive mountains rose abruptly from the rocky shore of the lake, and white creeks tumbled down the steep slopes. It was an intriguing and darkly mysterious lake. We decided to hike back and portage the canoe so we could explore this lake and the country beyond.

I lashed the paddles to the crossbars to make a carrying yoke, then Sally helped me lift the canoe onto my shoulders.

"If a moose challenges me, I'm ready!" I joked as I plodded up the first hill.

Stumbling along a narrow, winding game path with a cumbersome eighty-pound canoe balanced on my shoulders rates low on my list of enjoyable pastimes—very low. The unwieldly sixteen-foot canoe impeded my view of the narrow path, got tangled in trees, and seemed to grow heavier with each step.

"Your turn," I gasped after ten minutes of dodging branches and tripping over roots and rocks. Sally gamely took her turn, but lasted only five minutes before sagging to the ground under the weight. We each took one more turn carrying the canoe before finally reaching the small lake.

A long portage   *A pine squirrel*

A bull moose during rutting season

With our gear re-packed into the canoe, we pushed off to explore the lake which I had suitably named Portage Lake. It was a pleasure to be in the canoe again instead of under it! We paddled slowly around the lake, exploring deep bays and boulder-strewn inlets.

"Look, another path. This must be a moose highway!" I said, pointing to a well-worn game path which led through a wide draw. We pulled the canoe onto a rocky beach and followed the path towards the next lake. As Sally and I crested the top of a low hill, we encountered a breath-taking panorama. Below us was a sparkling, blue lake nestled in a wide, willow-lined valley. A white shoreline contrasted with the deep-blue lake, and autumn colours burned in waves of red, yellow and gold through the valley.

A beaver swam across the still lake, cleaving the reflected image of rugged peaks in two.

"It's beautiful," Sally said. "Let's call it Beaver Lake."

"That's really original!" I rejoined, but I couldn't think of anything better, so the name stuck.

Sally and I hiked down through a grassy meadow and found a sheltered picnic spot on the lakeshore. As we ate, we scanned the lake through binoculars. A long beach beckoned from across the water, and a shallow river flowed into the lake from a golden valley of willow and birch shrub. I would have liked to explore this beautiful lake by canoe, but a storm was building to the west. We reluctantly turned back; we still had a three-hour return trip by paddle and portage to reach our cabin.

Dark clouds scudded forebodingly across the mountain tops as we canoed across Portage Lake. Once at Hottah Lake we paddled furiously, hoping to reach sheltered water before the storm hit. But two miles of open water still lay between us and safety when a wall of dark, wind-driven water swept down upon us.

"Keep it into the wind!" I yelled as the first waves washed over the bow of the canoe. We followed the shoreline, struggling to keep the canoe directly into the wind, and pulling hard on our paddles; if we got caught sideways by the wind and waves the canoe could easily have capsized.

Sally was in the bow, and consequently had the most intimidating view as our small canoe plowed into the dark water. With each huge wave the bow lunged three feet into the air, then crashed down onto the lake, sending waves of icy cold water splashing over Sally and into the canoe.

Then the rain hit, blasting out of the dark sky and bouncing off the surface of the lake. The cold, driving rain stung our bare hands and faces. Sally glanced back at me for a brief moment—she was grinning from ear to ear through clenched teeth.

"Nice day, isn't it?" Sally yelled over the howling wind. It was a difficult physical and psychological battle to beat the oncoming waves, but I knew why Sally was smiling. She had won her personal battle not to give up, but to fight and find that extra energy she needed to keep paddling.

"We're almost there!" she yelled, "I can see the point."

We finally reached our sheltered bay after an hour of struggling against the wind, then rolled the canoe onto the beach and stumbled to the cabin. I was never more grateful at our foresight in keeping a stack of kindling by the stove than now, as I struggled to start a fire with cold-numbed and shaking hands.

Sally was shivering violently and showed signs of the first stages of hypothermia. We stripped off wet raingear and clothes and wrapped blankets around ourselves.

"What some people will do for attention!" I teased, trying not to show my concern as I fired up the small Optimus stove to make a hot drink. I handed Sally a steaming mug of hot chocolate, then checked her skin temperature and wrapped another blanket around her.

Sally gradually stopped shivering and her cheeks flushed red as she warmed up by the stove and sipped the hot chocolate.

"Let's see," I considered with a smile. "The books say the best way to warm someone is to share body heat!"

CHAPTER 11

Tucho Lake

By late September, frost on scarlet leaves reminded us that winter was approaching, and we were eager to explore and photograph new country before snowfall came. The winter woodpile and other chores could wait until poor weather.

"Where to next?" I asked as we studied the topographic map on our wall.

"Let's try hiking to Tucho Lake," Sally suggested, pointing to a long, curving lake twenty-two miles to the east.

My fingers traced an imaginary route across the map as I tried to visualize the lay of the land from the narrow contour lines, map symbols, and colours. I pointed out several marshes, three creeks, a river, and two mountains which lay between us and Tucho Lake.

"Minor details," Sally commented as we studied the map.

For the next six or seven days we would carry our home and possessions on our backs. We packed a tent, sleeping bags, clothes, cooking gear, food, and a few other essential items into our backpacks. Every item was weighed against its usefulness. I begrudged each ounce of gear and went to great lengths to cut down the weight of our packs: Toothbrush handles were cut off, toothpaste was repackaged into a film canister, food was of the dehydrated variety, and even toilet paper was rationed. We had learned the importance of lightweight travel the hard way, after too many trips lugging too heavy packs.

After paring down the weight of our packs to a minimum, eight pounds of camera, lenses, and a tripod seemed excessive. But the frustration of encountering a moose or some other animal and not having the camera would be worse than the discomfort of carrying the extra weight. With all of our food and supplies for a week, plus the camera paraphernalia, our packs each weighed about thirty-five pounds.

"Thirty-four pounds too much!" Sally said the next morning as she carried her pack to the canoe.

We paddled across Hottah Lake and up Intermittent Creek as far as possible, to reduce the miles we would have to carry our burdens. We pulled the canoe onto the shore, then shouldered our packs and hiked east along the creek bank.

The first mile of backpacking always seemed to be the worst, and this trip was no exception. Shoulder straps pulled unmercifully downward and waistbelts wore into our hips, but after an hour of trudging along, our bodies grew accustomed to the task and our burdens were forgotten in the excitement of exploring new country.

Once through the open marsh, we climbed up through thick willow shrub to a dense forest of spruce. I referred to the map occasionally to check our progress, and after three hours of hiking discovered that we had only travelled three miles. At this speed it would take us at least two days of steady hiking to cover the twenty-two miles to Tucho Lake.

"Your turn to be path-finder," I said, stepping aside to let Sally lead through the forest. Sally had an uncanny ability to find game paths. These paths made hiking faster and easier; without them we would have stumbled through blowdowns and thrashed through tangles of willow even more than we did.

Moose, deer, and wolf tracks left interesting stories in the soft mud of the game path. We stopped frequently to read the signs of previous travellers. On one trail we saw that a moose had suddenly broken into a run and swerved off the trail.

"What spooked him?" I wondered aloud.

"Look at this," Sally called from further down the path. "Maybe the animal that made these tracks scared the moose." She pressed both of her hands into the huge imprint; there was room to spare. We were sharing the trail with a grizzly. A *big* grizzly.

"Sure hope we don't meet up with that one," I said emphatically, "or if we do, I hope it's already had supper." We continued at a slower pace, making a considerable amount of noise to avoid any surprise meetings with bears.

The narrow path ended at a deep valley of willow and birch shrub. What followed was the most miserable mile of bushwhacking that I have ever experienced! It seemed that we became two miles tired for every mile travelled as we plowed through the six-foot-high mass of growth. Blindly, we pushed on, thrusting branches aside, stepping over tangles, and snagging our packs on branches. More than once Sally and I lost our footing when a pack-snatching tree caught us unprepared.

Through gaps in the willow growth we had occasional glimpses of the winding Tucho River far below us, glistening in the autumn-tinted valley like a silver ribbon woven through auburn hair. Red and orange shrubs coloured the avalanche chutes of rugged mountains like lava flowing down the dark sides of volcanoes. Far in the distance we could see the tree-rimmed depression of Tucho Lake.

We were in a photographer's paradise. Saw-toothed mountains bordered on sparkling, white glaciers, and pine forests carpeted the land in a soft, green plush. We stopped again and again along the way to capture a splash of colour, the blur of a waterfall, or an autumn scene on film.

"It would be a great picture if you stood over there by the creek," I suggested, pointing down a steep bank. Sally was used to being the subject of photos, and was usually patient while I fiddled with f-stops, filters, and lenses.

"Anything for a picture," Sally grumbled good-humouredly as she clambered down, still wearing her heavy pack.

"A little to the right," I called. "Not that far—a bit to the left, now.... Just a minute I have to change film!"

All too soon, the sun dipped behind ragged peaks, and we began our search for a campsite. We liked to allow at least one and a half hours to set up camp, gather firewood and water, and to cook supper. It was no fun to stumble around in the dark. The forest cooled off quickly once the sun had set behind the mountains, and we began to worry that we would not be able to find a comfortable campsite before nightfall.

With only an hour of daylight left we finally came to a suitable spot—a level moss-covered area, surrounded by spruce trees, with a creek nearby. Without wasting a moment of the fading light we heaved off our packs and began to set up camp.

After many trips together Sally and I had developed an efficient routine, and quickly attended to our tasks without discussion. We pitched the nylon tent together, then Sally unpacked and fluffed up the sleeping bags while I gathered dry underbranches of spruce trees for firewood. I went for water as Sally cleared an area for a small campfire, making sure to scrape down to bare earth in the moss-covered soil. By the time I returned, she had a campfire lit and ready for cooking.

"Great, when's supper?" I asked, slumping down onto the mossy ground.

"When you cook it!" was Sally's tired reply.

This was no time for a discussion of who's turn it was to cook—I was ravenous! I threw together a simple one-pot meal of instant noodles, tomato powder, and freeze-dried hamburger, then stoked the fire and waited impatiently for the mash to come to a full boil. This supper was exactly what we needed on backpack trips: it was fast to cook, nutritious, and even though it didn't look incredibly appetizing, at the end of a long, hard day it tasted almost like a gourmet meal. We sat on a fallen log, hungrily dipping our spoons into the pot. Over the course of many outings, we had worked out a system—the person who dipped the fastest, ate the most.

As darkness slowly draped the forest, Sally and I snuggled closer to the fire and each other. We sat in silence, enjoying the sounds of the forest. A gentle wind soughed in the treetops, the creek bubbled and gurgled soothingly, and our small campfire crackled cheerfully.

"Happy?" I asked.

"Completely. You know, I don't even know what day it is . . . or care."

We stayed up, talking quietly until the last glowing embers faded to dull red, then doused the coals and made our way to the tent by moonlight.

As usual, we spent the first few minutes in bed shuffling and shifting to find a comfortable position on the rough ground. I finally adjusted my body to fit the contours of the lumps and bumps under the thin mattress, with a rock positioned between my shoulder blades and a root nestled in the small of my back.

"Nothing short of an earthquake will get me out of this sleeping bag," I whispered, soon drifting into a deep sleep.

We were awakened abruptly the next morning by the sounds of a bear growling and prowling around our camp.

All that stood between us and our unseen visitor was the thin nylon wall of our small tent—not a very comforting thought. We felt frightened to be trapped in the tent, unable to see the bear, with no idea where it was or what it was doing. We could only hear its loud grunting and the crashing sounds it made in the forest as it circled our camp.

I suddenly realized how very vulnerable we were. It was a full day's travel back to our cabin. If we became hurt, no one would ever find us in this wild land. We had no gun or protection of any kind.

"Should we lie here and play dead?" Sally whispered hoarsely as we discussed our predicament. "Maybe the bear will go away."

"No, I'm going outside," I said. "At least then I can see the bear."

Nervously, I stuck my head out of the tent, half expecting to be face to face with a grizzly.

"No bear," I breathed, relieved at only hearing loud growls from the forest in the direction of our food cache. Fortunately, we always took the time to cache our food high in a tree away from camp, and never ate in the tent—a practice that paid off now. The enticing aroma of food in the tent could have meant an eight-hundred-pound dinner guest in the night.

I dressed and hesitantly crawled outside. Moving quickly, I started a fire with the wood we had set aside the night before. I added more and more pieces of wood until there was a large blazing bonfire. The grumping and growling continued as the bear circled our camp. I hoped the flames would keep the animal away.

We packed up camp in record time, jamming sleeping bags, tent, clothing and equipment into our packs. After putting out the fire, I nervously untied our food bag from the tree, then we hiked away. We moved slowly but deliberately, spurred on by the continuing growls of the bear.

It was more than an hour before pangs of hunger overcame our pangs of fear. We finally stopped by a creek to brew up a pot of tea and cook breakfast. Then, full of renewed courage and burnt porridge, we shouldered our packs and set off through the forest. Half a mile further we were dismayed by the sight of a roaring river, wildly coursing down the mountainside.

"Who put this river here!" I groaned. Few maps existed for this vast territory and the only one available was less than adequate; one inch on the map was equal to four miles. A half-mile-wide gulley was indicated by a mere eighth of an inch on the map, if it was represented at all, making our route-finding even more challenging. I looked at the topographic map again. It showed a valley, but no river at this location.

We reviewed our choices. Should we risk trying to cross the river? We could lose some of our irreplaceable gear in the torrent—or worse, one of us could be swept away.

Sally dipped her hand into the water. "It's cold . . . but I haven't had my morning bath," she said gamely. "Let's go for it!"

Using my pocket knife, I cut two dead branches off a tree for walking sticks to help us across the river. We removed our boots and pants, then plunged into the icy water.

"Yeaahh!" Sally yelled as we quickly but carefully picked our way across the deep boulder-strewn river. We soon discovered there was an art to crossing swift, frigid rivers; our legs wanted to rush across, but our feet had to take slow deliberate steps to avoid slipping. Our feet throbbed with pain from the searing cold water.

Sally always seemed to feel the cold more than I did. Once across the creek she sat on the bank, blinking back the tears which welled in her eyes, and biting her lower lip. Only at times like this did I remember that my partner was not always as strong as I was.

I gently warmed Sally's feet in my hands, then glanced across the river. "I think I forgot my boots on the other bank," I said mischievously. "Would you mind fetching them?"

By late afternoon we had almost given up hope of reaching Tucho Lake until the following day. Then we crested a hill and there it was, a beautiful aquamarine lake. We stood still, gazing. For the moment, we forgot about our heavy packs, sore feet, and tired bodies. The scenery was very different from Hottah Lake. Jagged mountains slowly rose from the wide valley, and the mighty, ragged Cassiar range dominated the eastern horizon. To the south, row upon row of high peaks led as far as we could see.

We pushed on towards the lake. Only one more mile, one more creek, and one more soggy stretch of marsh lay between us and our objective.

Low afternoon sun shimmered across the still surface of Tucho Lake as we reached an inviting meadow by the lakeshore. Clumps of alder, dressed in autumn gold, were scattered along the shoreline, and the still lake reflected the sharp outlines of nameless peaks.

"How about pitching our tent here?" I asked.

Sally didn't even answer; she just dropped her pack, flopped down where she stood, and nodded.

It was a perfect spot. We set up our tent facing the lake, then found small boulders to build a firepit. Even the fishing looked good here—trout surfaced lazily to feed on insects, leaving ever-widening rings on the still water.

Although I seldom seemed to have much luck fishing with just a line and lure, I rigged up a fishing rod with a willow branch and within fifteen minutes landed a fighting, flashing rainbow trout. We feasted on pan-fried trout and bannock baked over the fire. Supper had never tasted better.

Sally and I spent the following days exploring the open

Hiking to Tucho Lake

A creek crossing!

A grumpy black bear

valley around Tucho Lake. As we hiked through colourful willow glades, leaves of red and gold swirled around our legs, and frosted leaves crunched and crackled underfoot. Farther up the mountains, the cold nights had frozen the moisture in the ground, creating frost spires which poked up through the soil.

We could sense winter approaching while we camped at Tucho Lake. Strong breezes swept through the open valley each afternoon, sending frost-tipped leaves tumbling down. Evenings were cold enough to make a warm campfire welcome, and our second morning brought a thin shell of ice around the lakeshore.

On our third day we woke to the deep, sonorous music of trumpeter swans as they flew over the valley. It seemed as if their bugling calls were sounding taps for the summer which had passed. Thin, feathery clouds floated in the southern sky and by afternoon the sun was encircled by a halo of colours as it shone through the thin haze. The ring around the sun was a sure sign that the weather was changing. We decided to head home the following day.

We awoke the next morning to the soft plopping sound of wet snow falling onto the nylon tent. I looked out the tent door and saw the landscape plastered with white snow. Large wet snowflakes splattered onto the lake.

"Let's get going—we're a long way from home," I said, ruthlessly unzipping Sally's sleeping bag. I wanted to reach Hottah Lake before the snow became too deep for hiking.

To our relief, it stopped snowing by late morning; less than an inch had fallen and the game paths were still easy to find. We set a fast pace for the return trip, and were well over halfway home by the time we stopped to set up camp in a small meadow.

Later that evening, the veil of heavy clouds lifted to reveal a landscape draped in white. The full moon cast a silver-white light that flowed across the landscape like quicksilver, highlighting platinum-tipped trees. Crystals of frost decorated the forest and glittered in the moonlight like diamonds. It was such a beautiful, magical evening I wondered why we didn't camp out every night.

I discovered why the next morning.

"My boots are frozen solid!" Sally exclaimed as she tried

to squeeze her foot into a stiff boot. The only way to thaw the boots was to walk in them for half an hour while wearing only thin socks—a sure-fire method of waking up! Any remnants of sleep were rudely shocked from our systems by a creek-crossing only a quarter of a mile from camp.

As we hiked through the forest, we encountered a pungent odour. The smell gradually intensified until we reached the source—a large, muddy hollow.

"A moose mudbath!" I said as we skirted around the foul-smelling mudhole. Bull moose often urinated and wallowed in odorous baths like this one in hopes of attracting females with the fragrance.

"'Eau de Moose' is not my favourite," Sally said, wrinkling up her nose.

With all the distractions along the way I hadn't paid full attention to our route-finding. Through the last section of dense forest, we had not been able to see where we were headed and had lost our bearings.

"I don't remember this area," Sally observed with concern.

"Neither do I, but it looks like a nice enough place to be lost," I teased. I stopped and sheepishly took a compass bearing, then changed our route and headed due west, hoping that we would eventually come to the marsh of Intermittent Creek.

Fortunately, we soon reached the open marsh and followed the winding waterway towards the lake, but finding our snow-covered canoe on the white shore of the river proved to be almost impossible! Every snow-draped log or bump looked like a canoe to our weary eyes.

"Next time, I'll mark the spot with trail tape on a long pole!" I vowed when we finally stumbled across our canoe. If the snow had been any deeper we could have had a real problem, and I shuddered to think of the consequences.

It was a relief to finally slip the heavy packs off our shoulders. We savoured the sensation of weightlessness for the first minutes after removing our burdens.

"We made it!" Sally yelled, doing a jig with more energy than I could muster after a day of backpacking.

We paddled across the lake, then as we beached the canoe by the cabin, noisy Canada jays swooped from the trees and welcomed us home. Their usual cackling was replaced with a soft whistling.

"I think the little beggars missed us!" I observed.

"I think they missed our handouts," Sally countered.

It was great to be back at the cabin. After seven days of camping we appreciated the simple luxuries of our log home: a real table with chairs, a supper cooked on the wood-burning stove, and a shelter in which we could stand and walk about. But I think the nicest part of getting back to the cabin was being able to warm by the fire, then climb into the warm bed instead of a cold damp sleeping bag on the ground.

CHAPTER 12

Approach of Winter

"Get up, it's snowing!" Sally urged as she opened the cabin door.

"Mmph," I grunted lethargically from deep inside the warm sleeping bag. The weather had been a soggy mixture of rain and wet snow for the past week, and I could think of no valid reason to get up. It was Sally's turn to light the morning fire, and nothing, not even a new snowfall, would get me out of bed until the cabin was suitably warmed!

Just as I was drifting back to sleep, Sally slipped a cold, wet snowball under the covers. I yelled in shock, frantically threw the covers off, and leapt out of bed. By the time my feet hit the cold floor, I was fully awake.

"Now that you're up, why don't you have a look at the snow," Sally suggested.

Large fluffy snowflakes drifted down from the grey sky, almost like the downy feathers of geese that had flown over-head on their way south. The new snow overnight had trans-formed the landscape into a winter wonderland. Each branch of the willow bushes in front of the cabin was laced with sparkling crystals of white. It was only the middle of

October, but the gently falling flakes of snow signalled the approach of winter in our northern valley.

An incident later that morning was further evidence that winter was almost upon us. Shortly after Sally left the cabin for a visit to the outhouse, I heard a muffled scream. With morbid thoughts that a bear had surprised her, I frantically pulled on my boots and ran out the door carrying the gun.

I met Sally part way along the trail from the outhouse. "What happened?" I asked breathlessly.

She held up the frosty toilet seat and glared at the offending object. "From now on I'm bringing this thing inside to warm by the stove."

"Is that all? Is that what the screaming was about?" I asked peevishly.

"What do you mean, 'is that all?' I almost died of shock when I sat down!" she exclaimed. At Sally's insistence, we found a warm place above the stove to hang the toilet seat.

This was the season leading to "freezeup" in the north, when fingers of ice would stretch onto the ponds and lakes and gradually close the waterways in winter's cold grip. Each day we listened expectantly for the drone of Ron's floatplane that would mean he was bringing our winter food supply. We hoped he would come soon; a floatplane can only land on open water.

Freezeup was a long, slow process. First the swamps and small beaver ponds became sheathed in thin ice. Then, on clear, cold nights, we heard the soft, whispering sound of ice forming on the lake. But the lake didn't surrender to winter easily, and we often woke to a sound much like the harmony of chimes as the wind and waves shattered the thin sheet of ice into small crystalline shards.

It wouldn't be long before it was time to exchange canoe paddles for ski poles, and we wanted to photograph the soft white reflections of snow-draped scenery while the lake was still open. Thin ice crunched against the bow of the canoe and tinkled with each paddle stroke as Sally and I canoed to open water. Our destination was a shallow bay to the west where we had seen moose tracks on previous outings.

As we canoed along the frozen shoreline, the clouds lifted from the valley, uncovering a sparkling world of blue sky, white mountains, and snow-laden forests. Every tree and bush was draped in the white shawl of early winter. The grass along the shoreline was fringed with wet snow and hoarfrost glittered like diamonds on the low willow shrubs that hung over the lake.

We paddled quietly along the shore, watching for any signs of wildlife. As we entered the bay, Sally pointed to a marshy area on the far side.

"Moose!" she whispered. "You paddle ... I'll take pictures."

Although we had seen many moose through the fall, every new encounter was exciting for us. Each moose seemed to have a character of its own; this one was friendly and patient. The female stood calmly in the shallow bay, munching on underwater plants. Slowly, she looked up at us, water and strings of green plants streaming from her mouth.

"Any closer and we better start backpaddling," Sally whispered nervously as the moose exhaled loudly with a snort of steam from her flared nostrils. But the moose seemed to ignore us completely as we continued to take photographs. Sally even had time to change lenses and film before the moose felt we were too close and trotted away, taking long strides and splashing water high into the air.

When the large animal came to the thin shore ice I almost burst out laughing at her performance. The moose stepped on the ice and broke through, then stopped and pawed at the shelf and gingerly tried to walk on the ice again. After breaking through on her second attempt, she decided that the direct approach was more suitable and charged through the ice, splashing and splintering her way to shore.

Once on shore, the moose stopped and turned to look at us, had a leisurely pee, then wandered into the forest.

"Not shy at all," I said. "Did you get a photograph of that?"

Other outings were equally eventful during this exciting season. Another afternoon as we canoed along the lakeshore, we heard a faint *woo whoo, woo ho* carried on the wind from the north. We strained to hear the soft whistling chorus which sounded much like a woodwind orchestra. I scanned the horizon with binoculars for many minutes, then pointed to a ragged V of white wings on the northern skyline.

"I think they're whistler swans," I said.

The large, white birds passed above us heading southwest, then circled over the lake. We sat quietly in the canoe, hoping the swans would land on the lake, then watched with mounting anticipation as the flock circled lower and descended to the lake in unison. The majestic birds settled onto the water, talking among themselves in soft whistling tones that were much higher and more musical-sounding than the deep resonant voice of the trumpeter swans we had seen earlier in the fall.

Sally and I were as silent as possible as we canoed towards the flock of swans, but every time we approached to within camera range, they rose gracefully from the water and flew farther down the lake.

It was a memorable afternoon, watching the perfectly synchronized takeoffs and landings, the large white wings gliding on the wind. We followed the birds for more than an hour, but after many photographs of the swans taking off and landing and none of them sitting still, we decided a different approach was needed.

When the flock landed near a sandy beach, Sally and I quietly pulled the canoe onto shore. We slowly crept along the beach on hands and knees, then hid behind bushes to avoid being detected by the birds. At about one hundred yards we stopped and set up the camera and tripod. Our efforts were rewarded with photographs of the swans floating on the lake, their snow-white bodies reflected on the shimmering surface of the calm water. We were struck by the serenity of the composition, with the low sun highlighting the birds as they stretched and preened their long white wings. After I had taken only a few photographs, the birds must have sensed we were near and swam farther away from shore.

From the number of migratory birds that passed through the valley, it appeared that our lake was a resting area on a major flyway. When the weather was favourable, we took the opportunity to study and photograph many birds, including geese, ducks, and a host of shorebirds. A flock of fifty white-winged scoters floated in the bay by our cabin, noisy gulls held a beach party one afternoon, and we laughed as we watched awkward mallards skidding to a three-point landing on the frozen ponds, with feet outstretched and tails bouncing across the ice.

The resident loons at Hottah Lake mourned the ending of autumn with their wailing cry. One day we no longer heard their call; they had left for the winter. As other birds also left our valley we realized that winter would be a lonely, quiet season.

When the weather was too poor for photography, we stayed around the cabin and prepared for the cold season ahead. Our first and most important job was to cut enough firewood to last the winter. A well-stocked woodpile was as essential to our survival as it had been to the early settlers'.

Sally and I spent many long days cutting and hauling, then splitting firewood with axe and maul. We needed two kinds of wood for the winter: old, dry wood which would make hot cooking fires, and new, green wood which would burn slowly through the cold nights. For dry wood we cut down standing dead trees and hauled the logs to the cabin, where we sawed them into stove-length pieces and stacked them against an outer wall. For green wood we used the remaining sections of the trees we had cut when building the cabin.

This was a good time of year to split firewood. It was cool enough to work hard without overheating, yet warm enough to sharpen an axe outdoors without freezing our fingers. We enjoyed the physical work of splitting logs for our winter warmth, and watched with a simple pleasure as our woodpile grew to fourteen cords of neatly stacked wood.

Between spells of wood-chopping, I whittled a sliding latch and handle for the inside of the front door. We had thought of many designs for an inside latch which would also open from the outside, using cord, lever, or rod through the door. But each design had a significant flaw: if the mechanism broke or became frozen we would be locked out! We finally decided on a sliding latch inside, and another sliding bar outside. Locks were unnecessary—any visitor would be welcome to come into the cabin, as is the custom in the north—but a sturdy latch was needed to keep out uninvited animal visitors.

Other preparations for winter included collecting buck-

A friendly jay

Swans heading south

Last reflections before freezeup

ets of moss from under the trees where there was still little snow. We packed the moss into every crack between wall logs on the outside of the cabin, then did the same on the inside to keep out the cold winter winds. We'd had cold feet lately, even when the rest of the cabin was warm, so we banked snow around the foundation to keep drafts from seeping through cracks between the floorboards.

The animals and the few birds that remained in our valley were also preparing for winter. We hadn't realized how active the animals were around our cabin, until we saw new tracks after each snowfall: a bear had wandered by the cabin on its last stroll before hibernation, and wolf tracks led to the front door, then to the food-cache. We were shocked at how big the wolves were; long scratches from their claws reached nearly seven feet up the food-cache posts as the wolves tried to get at our food.

"I think we have a new visitor," I commented, pointing to a series of pigeon-toed tracks in the snow.

We compared our book of tracks to the impressions in the snow and decided that a porcupine had been snooping around the cabin. A pine marten had also visited, looking for scraps of food, and we saw the paired tracks of squirrels, who passed by as they searched for moss to line their nests.

The fluffy, grey Canada jays were more friendly and solicitous than ever as they fattened up for the winter. They waited for us near the front of the cabin each morning, and thanked us with soft mewing sounds when we placed food scraps on a stump. As soon as we turned our backs the camp robbers would swoop down on folded wings and gobble up the handouts, then fly off to nearby trees and store the bits of food in cracks and crannies, or under loose bark. One fat jay even took to hiding his food under the eaves of our cabin. The Canada jays were a noisy lot, screeching at each other and arguing over choice morsels of food.

We also heard many squirrels chattering and scolding in the forest. One morning my attention was drawn to an industrious squirrel collecting cones in a spruce tree beside the cabin. The squirrel was working at a frenzied pace, biting off and tossing cones from high in a spruce tree as he hung upside down or sideways, and jumped from branch to branch. After dropping a pile of cones onto the ground, the squirrel scurried down the tree and buried the cones one by one under the moss for his winter food supply.

"There's a squirrel outside who's averaging at least forty C.P.M.!" I told Sally when I returned to the cabin.

She turned to me with a puzzled look. "Forty C.P.M.?"

"Cones per minute," I explained knowingly.

But even the sassy squirrels and noisy jays grew silent as more snow fell in the valley during late October. Unlike the fat, lazy flakes which had floated down earlier in the month, these small flakes fell with a purpose, probably to announce that winter had truly arrived.

Each day was shorter than the last as the sun arced lower in the sky, barely rising above the high, snow-covered ridge to the south. By the end of October we no longer saw the sun, only its reflected light from behind the mountains.

The evenings of early winter had a beauty that surpassed that of any other season. On moonlit nights the forest was an enchanted world of tall, dark trees draped in white, and the lake was covered with floating crystals of ice which sparkled and danced in the moonlight. In the protected bay near our cabin a thin layer of opaque ice undulated with the small rolling waves, and dully reflected the white mountain peaks and sparkling stars.

On some evenings the northern lights played in the sky. It was an awe-inspiring light show. Shifting bands of chartreuse, green, yellow and red grew and ebbed in intensity. Long curtains of faint light twisted, turned, then disappeared into a dull, white haze.

With each cold night, the ice crept further onto the lake as Old Man Winter won the battle of the elements. The ice became thicker; winter's icy grip was only occasionally broken by a strong wind that drove plate-glass sheets of ice onto the shore like a scattered deck of cards.

In early November Sally and I went on our last canoe trip of the season. We bundled up in warm winter clothing and felt-lined Pak boots, then pushed the canoe out onto the ice. Two hundred yards of ice separated us from open water, and our progress was slow; Sally leaned over the bow, breaking the ice ahead of the canoe with her paddle, while I propelled us through the narrow passage until we reached open water.

We followed the ice-rimmed shoreline of the lake, then drifted part way down the Tucho River to see how freezeup was progressing. The gelid water ran slowly and the river was cluttered with chunks of floating ice. A small creek entering the river was completely covered with two inches of crystal-clear ice.

We beached the canoe, then crept onto the ice and looked down on the pastel-coloured rocks and sandy creek bottom two feet below us. It was an enchanting experience to lie on the ice and watch small green water plants waving in the gentle currents and tiny brown snails moving ever so slowly along the bottom. A brightly-coloured rainbow trout swam lazily by, oblivious of our presence, and we studied minuscule red or blue fresh-water shrimp through air bubbles in the ice which served as small magnifying glasses in our wintery window.

A droning noise suddenly interrupted our reverie. "A plane!" I yelled, jumping to my feet.

We scrambled across the ice, piled into the canoe, and paddled furiously back up the river to reach the lake. Because we saw or heard so few planes in our remote valley I felt certain it would be Ron.

"Faster!" I panted as we strained against the current. "Stroke, stroke!" I called to Sally, encouraging her to keep up the tempo as we paddled around the last corner to the lake, expecting to see a plane circling to land.

My heart sank as we watched the small plane fly across the east end of the valley, then disappear from sight. We sat silently, hunched over our paddles, neither of us wanting to be the first to say what we knew to be true—we probably wouldn't see our food before freezeup.

I finally broke the silence. "I hope Ron comes in the next couple of days, or it will be too late." The tension of waiting for the floatplane had become almost unbearable, not knowing if it would come today, tomorrow . . . or ever.

When we returned to our sheltered bay, we found that the passageway which we had broken through the ice two hours earlier was closed in with a film of ice. We crunched our way back to shore and pulled the canoe onto the beach. Within seconds of flipping the canoe over, feathers of ice formed and stretched over the bottom, until the the entire canoe was covered with a glaze of ice.

"Looks like canoe season is over," Sally observed.

That evening we turned on our single-sideband radio to try and get in touch with our pilot. With ice edging further onto the lake each night, time was running out. We hoped for the best with our Rube Goldberg improvisation of a portable radio wired to a pair of six-volt lantern batteries, and the antenna attached to a long pole with pieces of wire.

With the instruction booklet in front of me, I held the microphone in one hand and fiddled with the many knobs with the other. I tuned into a channel with a faint voice, then pressed the talk button.

"CQDX, CQDX," I said into the microphone, then listened intently to the small speaker. There was no response.

I continued calling, but only heard garbled voices in return. The radio was our only means of emergency communication with the outside world, and I found it hard to hide my feelings of despair from Sally.

"Let's save the batteries for another night," Sally suggested quietly. "Maybe we'll have better luck then."

CHAPTER 13

A Time of Isolation

"CQDX, CQDX, northern B.C. on the side. CQDX," I repeated into the microphone.

Each night, we tried to contact our pilot by radio, desperately hoping to reach him before freezeup closed the lake. Each night, the temperatures dropped lower and ice crept further onto the water as winter settled in our northern valley.

I tried the radio again. After many long minutes of fiddling with every knob on the appliance, I finally found a strong signal. We strained to hear the first outside voice that we had heard in almost two months.

"This is Kingfisher One, Tasmania, standing on the side."

I looked at the radio with disbelief, "TASMANIA?"

"It works!" I yelled into the microphone, then remembered the proper decorum for international radio communication.

"This is XM124482, western Canada, do you copy?" I asked nervously. We waited as the radio crackled and whined. Much to our surprise, the Australian radio operator heard us. I talked to him for a brief minute, then the voice faded under the noise of hissing and static.

We persisted for the next hour, trying different channels, then finally received another strong signal on the radio. I pressed the microphone button, "CQDX, northern B.C. on the side, B.C. 482." We waited in suspense for the voice to acknowledge us.

"Hello B.C. 482. This is Bud calling from Iowa, what's your location?"

I gave Bud our exact location and call letters, then waited for his response.

"Give me a minute, I'll rotate my antenna towards you," the voice crackled over the speaker.

"Go ahead B.C. 482."

"Bud, can you contact our pilot for us? We need supplies—soon!"

I paused for his reply.

Bud's faint voice came over the speaker. "Repeat.... Breaking ... up.... Re.... " Then the voice faded.

I jiggled every wire on the radio and batteries, fiddled with the knobs, and pressed the mike switch. "XM124482 standing on the side," I repeated over and over, then waited, desperately hoping to hear a voice in response.

We had hoped that Bud could relay a message to our pilot that we needed food and supplies, but our hopes were lost in the airwaves. The disappointment of having finally contacted someone, then hearing the voice fade away was almost more than we could bear.

"Maybe Bud will tune us in again if we stay on the air," I said to Sally, pretending optimism.

I kept calling on the radio for the next hour, trying to reach someone—anyone. Occasionally, we could hear faint garbled voices, but it seemed that no one could hear us.

After more than a week of trying the radio every night, we finally gave up. We felt more isolated, more lonely than we had ever felt before. The only hope we had left was that our pilot might still come in, but that likelihood grew slimmer each day as the ice stretched further onto the lake.

We waited, watched, and listened for the far-off drone that might mean our pilot was flying in with our winter food supply. We never gave up hoping until we woke one morning in mid-November to find the lake completely sheathed in ice. We had no idea why Ron hadn't flown in before freezup. Had the lakes frozen earlier than he expected? Was his plane being repaired? Had he crashed somewhere since we last saw him?

The seriousness of our situation finally became evident; we realized that without radio contact we were completely isolated in our remote valley. It would be impossible to hike across the high mountains, half-frozen rivers, and mile after mile of vast, untamed land to civilization. By land it was more than one hundred and twenty miles to the nearest settlement, and we were without enough food for the coming winter.

"I guess we're on our own," I admitted quietly.

"That's what we wanted, wasn't it?" Sally asked. "Now we can really test ourselves against the wilderness.... "

Sally and I spent the evening discussing our predicament. We had known when we came to Hottah Lake that we would have to rely on ourselves to survive, but we had placed too much faith in our radio and in our pilot bringing in food before freezeup. Even if Ron came now, he would have to make an air drop, and we were uncertain if the boxes would survive the drop intact.

"If we start rationing food now, and do our best to supplement our supplies with fish and grouse, we might be O.K." Sally suggested.

It sounded like a good plan. Fishing had been excellent through the summer and fall, and there seemed to be plenty of grouse in the forest. We started the next morning with high expectations of catching enough fish to last the winter. But fishing at below-freezing temperatures turned out to be much more difficult than during the summer and fall.

First, we had to hike along the frozen shoreline to the open river two miles away, then stand in near-freezing water to cast the line out. Next came the long wait for a fish to bite: cast out ... reel in ... cast out ... reel in. Then the line above water sprouted icicles and the rod guides began to freeze. So did the fisherman who was holding the rod!

For almost two hours, we took turns fishing, using different lures, trying to find the one most appealing to trout. But the fish had already slowed down their metabolism for the winter and it seemed they were not hungry.

Finally, a trout bit the lure. The fish arced out of the river, then dove straight to the bottom, pulling the tip of the rod almost to the water.

"Reel it in!" I shouted.

"I can't, the line's stuck!" Sally yelled as the fish leapt out of the water. Sally thought quickly, and dipped the rod into the water to thaw out the line, then began to reel the fish in.

"Now the reel's frozen," Sally gasped, as she tried to turn the small crank. I grabbed the slippery line with my bare hands and hauled the fish towards shore. As I struggled with the line, the fighting trout splashed out of the river, drenching me with icy water, then flopped into deeper water.

Sally stepped into the river to help, and water flooded over the top of her boots. She took a frantic sweep with the net, plunging her arm into the cold water, then on her second attempt finally landed our supper—a colourful twenty-inch trout.

It had been a cold, wet struggle for just one fish. Frozen beads of splashed water clung to our jackets, Sally's frozen sleeve and pantlegs became as stiff as cardboard, and by the time we hiked back to the cabin the fish had to be thawed before I could clean it.

"Well, at one fish per day, we should have our winter food by . . . next summer," I said.

We didn't have any greater success with grouse hunting. After two days of searching through the forest for grouse I finally found one hiding in a spruce tree—right behind the cabin. My elation at bringing home fresh meat turned to disappointment when we dined on the roasted grouse.

"BLECH—it tastes like a spruce tree!" Sally said. The grouse had been feeding on spruce needles, which gave it a strong and disagreeable flavour. With foul-tasting fowl, poor fishing, and the few wild plants and berries hidden under snow, our plans to supplement our winter food supplies had not worked out as we had hoped.

An early winter snowstorm kept us cabin-bound for the next three days as we contemplated our situation. Soft powdery snow sifted down like flour, blotting out the sights and sounds of the forest, and a heavy silence surrounded the cabin as the birds and small animals stayed in the shelter of the trees.

To keep from dwelling on our feelings of isolation, Sally and I busied ourselves by splitting firewood and working on other projects. We re-counted bags of flour, beans, and other supplies to see if we could stretch our provisions. Everything from candles, toilet paper, fuel and flour would have to be rationed. After many calculations, we came to the conclusion that even with strict rationing and a meagre menu of beans and bannock, we would not have enough food to last until spring. We had to obtain some fresh meat, and the only chance we had left was to hunt for a moose.

Neither Sally nor I had ever hunted large game before. I hesitantly took the old Lee Enfield rifle off the wall; we had hoped never to use the gun, and nervously prepared for our first hunt.

One of the reference books we had brought with us explained how to shoot and prepare big game. We carefully read all the instructions to be sure we would do everything right. Then Sally sharpened our small knives as I checked the gun over and made other preparations for the hunt.

We strapped on our snowshoes and headed into the forest early the next morning, tramping through six inches of new snow. The moose no longer fed at the marshes now, but wandered through the forest looking for food. Many had already left for lower valleys where winter browse was more available, but the new snowfall made it easier for us to follow the few animals that still remained.

By noon we found tracks in the snow. "They're from this morning!" Sally said as she bent down and felt the soft unfrozen snow of the impressions.

During the summer, we had learned to read tracks, and we knew that these broad, cleaved prints were made by a moose, probably a male because the prints were scuffed. We followed the trail through the forest for the rest of the day with no luck.

The next day was the same. We trudged through the forest following tracks that seemed to lead aimlessly in circles. I looked at Sally and smiled ruefully. "If there were a recipe for moose-track stew, we'd have it made."

Finally in the late afternoon we found a promising sign

in the meadows at the east end of Hottah Lake. The tracks led to a trampled area where a moose had pawed for food under the snow, and a depression in the snow indicated where the moose had rested. We made plans to return to this spot early the next morning.

By sunrise we were on our way back to the meadows. The ice on the lake was now thick enough to hold our weight, and we walked swiftly to keep warm in the five degree Fahrenheit temperature. When we arrived at the meadows, we found fresh moose tracks leading into the forest. Wolf tracks also criss-crossed the moose trail, indicating that we were not the only hunters with moose on our minds. We followed the tracks towards the inlet. Then, as we rounded a corner, Sally motioned for me to stop.

"There it is!" she whispered, pointing to the dark form of a young bull moose.

We slowly circled downwind from the moose so that it would not smell our scent. I loaded the rifle nervously, set the safety lever, and crept quietly up a small hill above the animal, knowing that if I missed this chance we might not have another.

I took a deep breath to calm myself, aimed along the open sights of the antiquated .303, then slowly squeezed the trigger.

Nothing happened.

I had forgotten to unlatch the safety lever. I was now unnerved to the point of trembling and had difficulty staying calm. "Quit shaking," I told myself in a low voice as I unlatched the safety, then took another deep breath.

Again I carefully aimed, held my breath, and squeezed the trigger. The gun recoiled against my shoulder and the shot echoed through the forest. For a moment I couldn't bring myself to look at the moose, but when I did I saw that, mercifully, my first shot had brought the large animal down.

Mixed feelings flooded over me. I was relieved that we no longer had to worry about our winter food supply, but the elation that hunters talk about eluded me. Instead, I experienced a strong feeling of sadness at having killed a wild animal.

Sally and I slowly walked towards the moose. "Where do

we start?" Sally asked, as we contemplated the gruesome chore ahead of us. We reviewed the booklet on butchering moose. Then I stood for a long moment staring at the moose, holding the small knife in my hand.

It took two long, nauseating hours to skin the carcass then clean and gut the large animal. The task of butchering the meat took another two hours; warm blood oozed down our sleeves, onto our pants, and down our white Pak boots as we carved roasts and steaks with the small knives. While I finished carving the meat, Sally wrapped each piece in aluminum foil and loaded our backpacks for the long hike home.

Our packs were so heavy that we had to help each other lift the weight to our shoulders. We trudged home slowly, bloodsoaked and weary, bent under the weight of our packs. I didn't know how much the packs weighed, but our canoe weighed eighty pounds, and the packs felt a hell of a lot heavier. With rest stops every fifteen minutes, it took us two hours to walk the two miles home.

"I'll never complain about a forty-pound pack again," Sally exclaimed when we finally reached the cabin. It took all of our remaining strength to haul the meat up the ladder to the food cache. We stumbled into the cabin, exhausted.

As we set about the simple tasks of lighting the fire and preparing supper, we felt an overwhelming sense of relief. For the first time in weeks we felt ready for the harsh winter ahead. Even though our supplies had not come in, we had all we needed for survival—a food cache full of meat, a large woodpile, and a warm cabin for the cold months to come.

CHAPTER 14

Blanket of White

By late November a calm silence had settled over our valley. The lake slept under a sheet of ice and a thick blanket of white snow, rumbling only occasionally as if turning over in its long winter slumber. More than a foot of snow muffled the sounds of the forest and smoothed the rugged features of the valleys, adding to the tranquillity and beauty of early winter. Daylight had dwindled to only seven hours of soft diffused light, followed by a long period of twilight as the low sun reflected off the white landscape.

"Let's sleep out under the stars," Sally urged after supper one evening.

On cold, clear nights twinkling stars dotted the sky, often accompanied by the ghostly glow of northern lights. Even though the temperature was a chilly five degrees below zero Fahrenheit, I agreed to spend the night out.

We stamped down a flat area in the snow with snowshoes, spread out a plastic tarp, rolled out our double sleeping bag and settled in for an evening of star-gazing. As our eyes adjusted to the darkness, the stars came alive, pulsing and burning brilliantly in the black velvet sky.

The Big and Little Dippers stood out clearly in the northern sky, and the Milky Way was a broad, twinkling path of luminescent light directly above us. We took turns looking through binoculars and referring to our star guide to identify the constellations. Looking towards the north we saw the constellation of Cygnus the swan, where the Milky Way split into parallel streams of faint light. Hundreds of other stars flashed red, blue, and white as they danced in the night sky above the high peaks.

Sally and I each made our secret wishes as the first falling star streaked from Cassiopeia, towards the northern horizon, taking a full minute and a half to complete its fiery journey. Light-years away, another shooting star seared across the southern sky.

Then, a faint glow started above the eastern horizon, like a thin cloud spreading across the sky, growing more intense each minute. The ever-changing curtains of waving colour became more radiant until the trees stood outlined against the purple-green glow of the *aurora borealis*. Suddenly, a white umbrella of light spread across the sky directly above us, pulsing brighter and brighter.

"It's just like a white swan with outstretched wings," Sally said.

We watched in awe as the rays arranged themselves into hundreds of shapes, and slowly merged to become curtains of light dancing in the heavens. As the boreal light-show faded, we snuggled deeper into the sleeping bag and pulled the drawstring tight, leaving only our noses exposed to the cold night air. Our frozen breaths swirled around us as we dreamily watched the last colours of the aurora dissolve into the black sky.

"It's so peaceful," I whispered as Sally edged closer to me. We drifted off to sleep with an overwhelming sense of well-being. To lie out on a calm, quiet evening like this was to feel that all was well with the world, at least within our wilderness realm.

Sally nudged me awake in the middle of the night. "Listen," she said. "Wolves!"

From part way up the hill near our cabin came the low howl of a timber wolf. More wolves joined in, starting on a high note, then slowly dropping in tone and volume.

Ow, Ow, Owwhoo-oo-oo. The musical, mournful call echoed in the still air. This was the time of year when wolves roamed in packs, and the hunting call we heard sent shivers down my spine. Yet, in their own way, the wolves made haunting, harmonious music. The wavering howls became louder and more intense as the pack passed behind the cabin.

"Do you want to go inside the cabin?" I asked.

"No, I wouldn't want to miss this—even if I am a little frightened," Sally whispered. The last sound we heard before falling asleep was the faint call of wolves from the west end of the valley.

A low growl woke me early the next morning. I remembered the wolves we had heard in the night and my first thought was an unsettling one: "Here I am, all trussed up in a sleeping bag like a wrapped roast."

The low, ominous growl came again, this time even closer to where we lay.

"Ian!" I heard Sally hiss from inside the sleeping bag. Nervously, I stuck my head out of the bag. Without my glasses I could only see the vague outline of a dark animal as it slowly, stealthfully approached us. I tensed with fear as the animal growled again.

As my eyes adjusted to the dim light I saw the fearsome animal—the small, mischievous pine marten that often visited our cabin was stalking us from six feet away. I chuckled at the thought of pouncing on Sally and letting out a loud roar, but decided that she would not appreciate the joke.

"It's only the marten," I whispered.

Sally poked her head out just in time to see our furred visitor bound into the forest.

"He got us again," Sally said laughing.

It had been a cold night, and white frost encircled the opening of our sleeping bag where our breaths had frozen. We crawled reluctantly out of the warm bag and dashed to the cabin. After thawing out by the warm stove with mugs of hot coffee and breakfast, we decided to take advantage of the clear weather and go skiing.

The aroma of camp coffee mixed agreeably with the scent of hot ski wax as I prepared our skis for a trip to the high country. Sally loaded extra clothing, food, first aid and emergency equipment into our packs. These extra items made our packs heavy, but they were essential for safe winter travel; we had to be fully self-sufficient and prepared for any emergency wherever we ventured.

Soft snow swished ahead of our skis as we glided through the forest behind our cabin. We climbed up through the trees to Grouse Ridge, teased by tantalizing glimpses of the sparkling-white landscape and blue sky through snow-laden branches. After more than an hour of skiing, we finally reached the open alpine slope.

The scenery was spectacular. Rows and rows of white ridges and peaks massed in the distance, with more peaks at every turn. To the south, two rugged mountain ranges thrust skyward from peaceful white valleys, and the high flat Spatsizi Plateau stretched to the horizon line. Looking west, we could see the dark line of the Tucho River, which had still not completely frozen. In the opposite direction lay the snow-covered bowls of Portage and Beaver lakes, joined by a thin band of ice. Hottah Lake was directly below us in the blue winter shadow of mountains, but where we stood bright sunlight flooded across the slope, sparkling on the newly fallen snow.

"I could stand here all day," Sally said, scanning the horizon.

"I couldn't," I replied with a shiver as I photographed the landscape. "It's too cold!"

Even though the sun was brilliant, it radiated little warmth. A cold wind buffeted the open slope and ice had already formed on my beard. We dug a pit in the snow and bundled up in all the clothing we had brought to keep warm. We had hoped to enjoy the view for a while, but we could only pause long enough to share a thermos of hot tea and a handful of trail mix before we became cold.

We started down the mountain, cautiously carving our first wide turns of the season. It took only a few turns to get our ski legs back. We soon became more aggressive and soared down the steep slopes, floating on the powder snow. Sally and I carved telemark turns, crossing each other's tracks, whooping and hollering as we gained confidence and speed.

Sally scored the first wipeout of the season, cheered on by a most appreciative audience of one.

"Encore, encore," I hooted, as she glared at me from a horizontal position.

"Are the cameras O.K.?" I asked, feigning worry.

"Cameras—is that all you think about? What about me?" Sally asked, tossing a snowball.

"You? Oh yeah, maybe I should give you some ski lessons!"

Shortly afterwards I executed one of my famous double-roll, triple-summersault, twisting half-gainer headplants. The soft snow was most forgiving, although it took considerable effort to extricate myself from the depths.

Nothing was damaged but my pride. I looked up to see if Sally had seen my wipeout. "Good," I thought, "she's still skiing." I quickly removed snow from behind my glasses, from inside my ears and around my neck, and brushed it off my clothes. Then I skied down to catch up with Sally.

She was far ahead of me, carving turns around, under, and between the trees. Gamely, I tried to follow her obstacle course down the mountain, dodging trees, branches and bushes.

"You seem to have a lot of snow clinging to your clothes," Sally jeered when I finally caught up to her.

"Merely snow thrown up from the speed of my descent," I countered.

Further down, the trees grew too close together to negotiate at speed. Rather than risk catching a ski on a branch or crashing into a tree, we prudently took off our skis and walked the last half mile to the cabin.

That evening the temperature plunged to fifteen below zero, and the following days of early December were clear and cold. We turned our attention to insulating the cabin to keep out cold drafts: repacking loose moss between wall logs because the logs had shrunk in the cold, and banking more snow around the foundation and lower wall logs for insulation. We also tacked plastic sheeting over the windows to keep the cabin warmer, and stuffed an old pair of jeans along the bottom of the door to keep out drafts.

The weather was too cold for us to ski to the high country. Instead, we stayed closer to home, exploring along the

The high country *Snowshoes and solitude*

The cabin blanketed with snow

frozen waterways and snow-covered meadows of the valley. On clear, cold days towering white mountain peaks crowded around us; even distant mountains seemed to loom at the very end of Hottah Lake, and the nearest ones appeared so close that it seemed we could reach out and touch them.

One of our favourite outings was to ski across the frozen surface of the lake. It was a wonderful feeling to speed along the smooth, windblown snow—kick, glide, kick, glide, in fluid rhythm. We felt a sense of freedom and exhilaration as we skied; there were no willow bushes to scramble through, no swamps to wade across, or scrub spruce to tangle with— only the smooth white covering of winter.

We went skiing almost every day, except during the worst snowstorms. After each snowfall fresh animal tracks punctuated the landscape, and we often followed them to see where they led. Reading the tracks was like reading a good book, with a new chapter after each snowfall. Every change of pace and every detour told an exciting story of the animal's life.

On one trip we followed the dotted line of wolf prints along the north shore of the lake. The wolves followed in each other's tracks, and we sometimes saw where the first wolf stepped aside to change lead position with another wolf. Occasionally a set of prints veered away from the worn path, where a wolf had changed course to investigate something of interest, or to sprinkle a rock to mark the pack's territory.

The wolves had turned onto a winding creek where they joined the tracks of a moose. Around the next bend we noticed a change of pace; the wolf tracks fanned out to four abreast, and we could tell by the length of strides that they had started to run. Splayed out hoofprints showed the moose was fleeing from the wolves.

Sally and I followed the trail like two eager detectives looking for clues. The plot became more intriguing as we followed the tracks to an open meadow. It became a tempestuous story of survival in the wilderness as we found slurred tracks, patches of moose fur and bright red spatters of blood on the snow. We saw signs of a scuffle. Then the tracks turned into the forest.

Our heartbeats quickened as we speculated about the

fate of the moose. We continued slowly, not sure if we really wanted to know the outcome. The wolves had followed the moose only a short distance into the forest. Then they had veered away from the moose tracks, and slowed to a trot. It looked as though the moose had been able to outrun the wolves in the trees and escape.

Other stories in the snow were less dramatic, but just as interesting. On another outing we were puzzled to find long, narrow troughs in the snow, which led towards the open water of Tucho River. Further on we could see where a small animal had bounded along the snow-covered ice, slid for six to eight feet, run a few more paces, then slid again. The tracks continued for almost half a mile to where the animal finally slid into an open pool of water by some rapids.

"Looks like fun," I teased, grabbing Sally by the arm. "Want to take a slide into the water?"

"Quiet!" Sally said, elbowing me and pointing down the river. "Look over there." In the distance I could just make out a small dark form moving across the broken ice.

We skied closer, then from behind some bushes I photographed a sleek black otter frolicking at the edge of the ice. The playful otter seemed to pay no heed to the cold weather as he slid down the bank into the river, swam around, then climbed up to the top of his slide for another run. He was having a great time, sliding down on his stomach, then rolling over onto his side as he splashed into the icy water.

As we watched the otter play, we came to realize that even in the wild, winter was not all hardship and violence. Many animals took time out from their search for food to enjoy a frolic in the snow. In a way, we felt a kinship with the otter. Our life was also rugged, but we had learned to enjoy the simple pleasures of winter—the quiet, cold days, the clear, starry nights, and the freedom of skiing across the white winter landscape.

CHAPTER 15

Cabin Life

The thin red column in our low-registering thermometer dropped lower with each cold, clear night. As temperatures plunged below minus twenty, the usual silence of the forest was shattered by the booming of freezing sap bursting the inner fibers of trees and the thundering of expanding lake ice buckling in the cold.

We could usually guess the temperature outside our cabin even before we climbed out of bed each morning. The rough-hewn front door of the cabin served as a fairly accurate thermometer: if there was frost along the bottom of the door, the temperature was around zero degrees Fahrenheit; hoarfrost a foot up the door showed it was below minus ten; and white rime halfway up the door indicated minus twenty.

I looked from the bed one morning in early December and saw a thick layer of frost covering the entire inside surface of the door. Not an encouraging sign. Then a cabin log beside the bed boomed loudly, abruptly waking Sally from a deep sleep.

"What was that?" she yelled, springing upright.

"A log freezing—and it's your turn to light the fire before we freeze too," I answered, pulling the top of the sleeping bag over my head.

We lay in our warm sleeping bag debating whose turn it was to light the fire for many minutes before I conceded, "O.K., first one to get up lights the fire."

Finally, Sally decided to get up. "Just goes to show who has the greatest strength of character," she muttered as she squirmed into clothes while still under the covers.

"I'd say it has more to do with weakness of bladder!" I replied.

I lay in bed, listening sleepily as Sally performed the morning ritual of rekindling the fire. I could imagine every step, for I had done it a few times myself when Sally's bladder held out longer than mine. First came the metallic creak of the stove door being opened, then silence as Sally carefully stacked wood chips and kindling in the firebox. Next came the scratch of a match across the front of the stove, followed closely by the sound of Sally blowing on the fire. Then came the snapping and crackling of burning wood, and finally the rhythmic ticking of the stovepipes as they slowly warmed up.

A little while later the stove door creaked again, and a dull thud and sizzling hiss of sparks came from within the stove as Sally threw another log onto the fire. With a splash, the coffee pot was dipped into the water bucket, and then set, spluttering, on the hot stove. Finally came the splosh of a handful of coffee grounds being tossed into the cold water to slowly come to a boil—camp-coffee style. I decided that this was my cue to get out of bed.

Although it had been only a few minutes since Sally lit the fire, the fragrance of burning pine made the cabin seem warmer. As I dressed, the keen aroma of coffee drifted across the cabin.

"Where's the toilet seat?" I asked, when I didn't find it hanging in the usual place of honour behind the stove.

"Sorry, I left it at the outhouse," Sally replied, with very little hint of remorse in her voice. In fact, I'm almost sure I noticed a slight, wicked smile being kept back.

I paused to check the thermometer on the way. Minus twenty-seven degrees. "Great. . . . The coldest morning ever, and she leaves the seat outside," I grumbled to myself.

The dry snow squeaked and crunched underfoot as I walked along the path beside the cabin. At first the dry air didn't feel as cold as the thermometer indicated, but within a minute the tip of my nose began to tingle and cold air seeped into my down jacket. It seemed like a good morning to stay inside the warm cabin.

Our mornings were usually spent around the cabin, taking care of the many chores of our rustic life. Fetching our day's supply of water involved breaking through thick ice over the water hole with an axe or peavy, then hauling heavy buckets of water up the steep, icy trail to the cabin. Sometimes we slipped and had to return to the lake for more water. To keep the fire burning day and night we had to maintain a constant supply of firewood. Splitting logs was a time-consuming task, but an enjoyable one; it provided a good opportunity to work out our frustrations. During one wood-chopping session I think I heard Sally muttering something about getting up first in the morning, then driving the maul deep into a large block of wood.

In addition to splitting four to six armloads of wood each day to heat the cabin, we also split one or two armloads for cooking and baking. A special combination of both wet and dry wood was needed to maintain just the right temperature for the forty minutes it took to bake bread in our stove-top Coleman oven. To control the stove's temperature, we had to constantly tend the fire and fiddle with the damper and air vent. Baking cookies and muffins in the reflector oven was just as difficult; it was a challenge to cook the back row of cookies sufficiently without burning those in the row closest to the stove.

A morning each week was set aside for laundry. Winter washdays were even more tedious than summer washdays. It was a lengthy task to haul buckets of water from the frozen lake, and the near-freezing water took a stubbornly long time to come to a boil. We had to stoke the fire every few minutes, and it took almost three hours to heat the water.

Next came the backbreaking task of washing the dirty clothes using my mother's patented plunger-in-a-bucket method. The cabin was filled with the musty smell of wet wool and the scent of soap as we washed thick socks, long underwear, and wool shirts. After scrubbing, plunging, rinsing and wringing, the clothes were hung outside to dry—that is, to freeze-dry. After most of the moisture had evaporated, we brought the frozen scarecrow silhouettes inside to thaw and finish drying.

With the laundry out of the way—actually, it was in the way, with woollies hanging from clotheslines strung across the cabin—we turned to other projects.

"How about making REAL chairs?" Sally suggested one morning. "These hard wooden stumps are a pain in the rear!"

Our first creation was a chair made from poles, complete with a back and seat strung with a latticework of nylon rope. Although the chair did not look sturdy, it did look elegant. Remembering the bruises my body and ego had suffered in testing the bed, I offered Sally the honour of trying the chair first.

"You're heavier," Sally countered. "I think you should try it first."

I held my breath and sat down gingerly. Nothing broke! I tried not to look too surprised, then settled down more comfortably into the chair.

"This is great," I sighed . . . a millisecond before the chair burst apart and I collapsed to the floor.

A better design followed, modelled after a director's chair; it featured thicker poles, more nails, and a sturdy canvas back and seat. The chair was durable and so incredibly comfortable compared to the stumps that we decided to spend the next day building another.

After our morning chores were completed, I usually spent some time writing while Sally sketched or worked on her wood carvings. I often found inspiration for writing in the ever-changing views of the lake, forest, and mountains which were framed by the cabin windows. No matter how blankly I sat, staring out the window, I could often count on some playful bird or animal to enter the scene and motivate my pen with its antics.

Our most frequent visitor was a squirrel who came to the front window to beg for granola. One day the small creature put his front paws on the window and pressed his nose against the plastic like a child looking in through a candy store window. I couldn't resist his antics, and opened the door to offer my visitor some breakfast. The squirrel bounded eagerly towards the door and settled down only three feet away to munch on the granola I had thrown out.

On another occasion, as I was writing in my journal, our resident marten peered in the side window of the cabin. The marten was a pretty, graceful animal with bold, gleaming eyes, black whiskers and a tiny black nose. His dark brown coat sported a cream-coloured strip along his belly and a bright splotch of orange on his chest. Since any excuse was enough to entice me away from my writing, I watched the marten intently until he bounded back into the forest.

After writing for one or two hours, I was usually ready for some fresh air and exercise. Even on days when the weather was poor or temperatures were very low, we went on outings. It had become too cold to ski, but we donned felt-lined Pak boots and snowshoes to explore our white environment.

One afternoon we trudged to the beaver pond east of the cabin. The beaver lodge was now no more than a snow-covered mound on the featureless pond; crystals of hoarfrost encrusted the small breathing hole. Wolf tracks led around and over the small hill, but the beavers inside the lodge were safe from the cold and their enemies.

From the beaver pond, we moved on through sparse forest to the Tucho River. We were surprised to find areas of open water remaining on the river, but the rapids were still flowing too swiftly to freeze over completely. At the bottom of each set of rapids were thick pieces of ice piled high in jumbled masses.

We walked back upriver, then headed homeward along the shoreline of Hottah Lake. Suddenly, a beautiful silver-grey timber wolf appeared on the shore and stopped to look at us.

Our first wolf sighting! We had read about wolves and had heard them, but we had never seen them except in photographs. The large wolf was a beautiful animal with a thick ruff of dark fur around its shoulders. We watched quietly as the wolf twitched its large ears, then lifted its nose to get a scent of us. As long as we stood still the wolf remained watching us, but as soon as I moved to get the camera out of my pack, the animal trotted away.

"That was really something!" Sally exclaimed happily as we snowshoed back to the cabin. "I've always wanted to see a wolf. Did you see those piercing, green eyes?"

We arrived at the cabin just before three o'clock. Dusk was already settling over the valley. After a few hours of snowshoeing in the frigid, frosty weather, Sally and I were ready to go inside and stoke up the fire for a cozy afternoon of reading, writing in our journals, and other indoor pastimes until supper.

Our favourite supper was moose stew with reconstituted vegetables, and rice. Moose steaks, roasts and liver still seemed like treats, after the months we had spent subsisting on Prem and freeze-dried hamburger. We were eating well, but, because our supply plane had not arrived, we still had to ration some supplies. With a limited selection of staples to work with, it was a challenge to create a variety of appetizing meals. One evening I had a sudden urge for a pizza. I created a camp-style pizza using bannock for a crust, and topped it with tomato powder, lentils, dried vegetables, moose meat and cheese. Other evenings we had a choice of spaghetti, macaroni, baked beans, or soup.

After supper we often spent our evenings playing rousing card games, with the loser having to wash the dishes.

"You lose!" I exclaimed the first time Sally dropped a card and it slipped through a crack in the floor.

"Only if I can't find it," Sally protested as she peered through the floorboards. She spent half an hour looking for the card, then conceded it was lost and did the dishes. From that night on, a piece of cardboard served as the seven of clubs.

Cribbage was my favourite game, and for good reason: by December the tenth, the running total stood at—Ian 241, Sally 63. After each win I rubbed in the fact that I was a superior crib player.

"How does it feel to be skunked again? Pee-Yoooo!" I teased. By December the fifteenth my taunting finally became too much for Sally.

"I'll play rummy, poker, or chess . . . but no more crib for a month!" she said in frustration.

A winter washday

Fetching water

A quiet evening in the cabin

Quieter evenings were spent near the warmth of the fire, reading by the yellow glow of kerosene lamp-light. We had brought in almost two hundred paperback books, ranging from Shakespeare plays to reference works on outdoor topics. Two bookshelves occupied the southwest corner of the cabin. One shelf held the outdoor books, medical manuals, photography handbooks, cookbooks, and a dictionary and thesaurus. The other shelf contained fiction and non-fiction paperbacks, classics, and a book of Robert Service poems about the north.

The pace of our lives had slowed to a pleasant routine, and we always seemed to have plenty of diversions to fill the long evenings. One evening I spent more than two hours assembling a difficult jigsaw puzzle—a rounded glass globe of the kerosene lantern which had fallen off the table. I painstakingly fitted together the eighteen-piece, clear, three-dimensional puzzle with epoxy glue. It rivalled any two-hundred-piece puzzle in difficulty and aggravation.

The greatest disaster that can happen to a jigsaw puzzler is to discover that the last piece of the puzzle is missing. And, as I fitted the last pieces together, it became obvious that this misfortune had befallen me. Sally and I searched every inch of the cabin floor. I finally spotted the missing piece—it had fallen through a crack in the hewn log floor and lay on the ground twelve inches below. There seemed to be no way to retrieve it.

I knelt over the crack, pondering the best way to tackle the problem. Finally, I lowered a splinter of wood coated with honey and after minutes of fishing around by the light of a candle, the glass stuck to the honey on the wood. Slowly . . . ever so slowly, I raised the glass through the narrow crack.

It took only an hour to finish the puzzle once I had reclaimed the missing piece. The final product was, if not perfect, at least functional; the kerosene lantern simply would not have worked without the glass globe.

A highlight of each week was bath night. In the late afternoon we would venture to the lake for six buckets of water. While we fed dry wood into the stove and watched the steam rise from the water pails, we would debate whose turn it was to take the first bath. One evening when we couldn't agree on who would have the first bath, we decided to have one together. The tub was too small to allow us to bathe very effectively—but we sure had fun!

After waiting in anticipation for many hours while the water heated it was a real treat to lie in the tub beside the warmth of the woodburning stove. Pure luxury! We enjoyed our weekly baths, even though the tub was only large enough to allow the occupant to sit upright in a cross-legged position, or to lie back with legs hanging over the end. There was not even enough room to scrub our own backs. So, baths became a shared event with help from a "scrubber", whose other duties included keeping the stove warm and heating stones to drop into the tub as the water cooled down.

By nine or ten o'clock each evening we had used up our ration of six hours of lantern fuel. Before going to bed we would cross the day off the calendar and wind the clock. We had forgotten to cross off a day on occasion and had lost track of time many months ago, but we persisted in these rituals to maintain some sort of connection with our city lives.

Another pre-bedtime routine was to set the mousetraps. At first we hadn't minded our pet mouse or the few relatives who came along, but when its large grey cousins started to visit we were forced to set the traps: with our limited supply of food, we couldn't have mice helping themselves. We even had to ration the amount of cheese we put in the mousetraps!

The last chores of the day were to cut wood shavings and kindling, to stack dry firewood neatly by the stove, and to fill the firebox with large green logs. After stoking the stove at night, the fire would burn well into the morning hours. As long as the outside temperature dropped only to thirty below, the cabin would still be a comparatively cozy plus-forty degrees come morning.

As the thermometer dipped further, we began to think about getting up during the night to tend the fire. One particularly chilly evening, I remembered having heard of an old sourdough method of ensuring that the fire didn't go out. To be sure that they would wake up in the night to tend the fire, the trappers would down three to four large glasses of water before bedtime. They would then sleep until na-

140

ture's alarm clock woke them in the middle of the night. After attending to the most urgent function, they would sleepily rekindle the fire that had flickered out in the night.

I filled the firebox with as much wood as I could fit in, closed the damper so the fire would burn slowly, then graciously offered to bring Sally a large mug of tea in bed.

"By the way," I hinted as Sally sipped her tea, "if you're up first, would you mind lighting the fire?"

CHAPTER 16

A Wilderness Christmas

Santa arrived at Hottah Lake in a blue-and-white Cessna 185 on skis!

I was out for a short afternoon ski to the east end of the lake when I heard the distant drone of a plane. A few minutes later a small ski-plane flew up the valley, then landed on the lake near the cabin.

I turned around and raced back towards the cabin. My lungs burned and heart pounded from the effort of skiing so fast in the cold weather, but I desperately wanted to get to the cabin before our visitor left. Then I heard a roaring sound, and watched with dismay as the plane took off.

"Damn! Our first visitor in four months and I'm out skiing." I stopped and leaned on my ski poles, feeling frustrated and disappointed.

The Cessna flew low over the trees then turned and flew back up the valley towards me. I couldn't believe my eyes when the plane banked sharply and descended to the lake. It landed beside me in a flurry of soft snow. I could see our pilot Ron smiling broadly as he flung open the small door.

"Merry Christmas!" Ron shouted over the noise of the

engine. "Climb in, I'll take you to the cabin. Sally was worried you'd freeze your lungs racing home."

As I put the skis in through the door, Ron cautioned me to watch out for the propeller. "The skis would kinda be chewed up. Wouldn't do the prop much good either," he added.

We taxied down the lake to the cabin. As we climbed out of the plane Sally ran up and gave Ron a big hug. "That's my second hug! Guess you haven't seen anyone for quite a while," Ron said, with a shy grin. "Sorry I'm a little late. The lakes froze early this year and I had to wait to get my plane on skis."

We stood on the lake for some time just talking. When Ron began stamping his feet to keep warm we remembered our manners and invited him into the cabin for tea and bannock.

"Do you know what day it is?" I asked, as we walked to the cabin.

Ron laughed, then replied, "The nineteenth . . . of December, that is. How many days have you lost?"

"Only two, I think!"

Ron's eyes roamed around the small cabin as we entered the front door. This was the first time he had seen our completed home, and he seemed impressed with our craftsmanship and furnishings.

"Your parents and I were worried about you two—nobody has heard from you since the summer," Ron commented.

"We're doing O.K. so far, but our radio quit after one call," I said.

"Well, I guess if you've survived this long, you should be able to look after yourselves 'till next summer," he reassured us.

Ron listened intently to our stories of wolves, freezeup, and winter life. We learned that Ron had spent part of a winter in a remote cabin, so he understood what our life was like. The only difference between his situation and ours was that he'd had a ski-plane handy and a radio that worked.

The time passed all too quickly and as dusk began to darken the sky, Ron prepared to leave. The plane's engine turned over hesitantly in the minus-thirty-degree cold. But after some coaxing, it fired up. As the Cessna taxied out of our bay the propeller sent clouds of icy snow whirling back, forcing us to duck for cover. We couldn't hear Ron's words, but we knew he was shouting "Merry Christmas" as he wagged the plane's wings and flew over the lake.

We quickly turned our attention to the boxes Ron had brought in. They contained our much-needed winter food supply and extra goodies we had packed for our Christmas celebration. Like two children, we ripped open the boxes to see what we had packed seven months earlier. Fruitcake! Mince! Candy canes! A frozen half-bottle of champagne!

"No more rationing!" I exclaimed. "What a fantastic Christmas present."

Ron had also brought in a shopping bag crammed full of letters, parcels and presents. Sally and I spent the rest of the evening sorting and reading through the bag of letters. Some had been mailed as long ago as August. We sat on the bed with a pot of tea beside us and arranged the letters in chronological order, according to the postmarks. Then we packed four months of news and excitement into four hours as we read reports of weddings, birth announcements, and other family news.

The letters contained such teasing remarks as, "Well, it's time to take a bath—I guess I shouldn't have mentioned BATHTUB, eh? It might remind you of hot water (running), bubblebath and other stuff like that! Oops!" A friend with a rather bizarre sense of humour sent us movie schedules and takeout menus from pizza parlors and Chinese restaurants, just to give us a "dose of civilization." And another friend, not knowing when we might get her letter, summed it up by saying: "If this gets to you by Christmas I hope you both have the very happiest ever, and if it gets to you by New Year's I hope the same, and the same again if it reaches you by Easter. Or . . . Happy Birthday if this arrives next summer!"

After reading all the Christmas cards and letters we felt a strong spirit of Yuletide. The next morning we went snowshoeing in the forest to find a Christmas tree for the cabin. Searching for the ideal tree was not an easy task—there were thousands to choose from. We snowshoed through the deep snow and stopped at each small, snow-laden tree, shook the snow off, and sized it up. I'm not sure whether our standards dropped, or if we indeed found the perfect tree, but, after an hour of tromping around in minus-thirty-five-degree weather, we finally agreed on a spruce tree which we took home.

"Let's make our tree a gift to the birds and animals after Christmas," Sally suggested as we discussed how to decorate the tree. We felt a certain affinity with the animals that shared the harsh winter with us, and we decorated the tree accordingly, with strings of popcorn, kidney beans, and raisins. Dried apple rings, other dried fruit and pieces of salami hung from branches.

We made other simple decorations for the tree from pieces of aluminum foil, strips of red cloth torn from an old shirt, and sections of toilet paper rolls painted red and green. Sally painted cabin decorations with her water-colours, and we fashioned a wreath for the front door by tying spruce boughs in a circle and decorating it with a bow made from red trail-marking tape.

During the days before Christmas, Sally and I became more and more occupied with special projects, the kind that had to be quickly hidden away when the other person returned to the cabin. Sally would offer to leave the cabin so that I could be alone "to write," and she would ask for time by herself "to draw." It took some imagination and resourcefulness to make presents from what the forest had to offer; I spent almost an hour one afternoon looking for the right-shaped branch with which to make a double coat-hook for Sally.

"Don't come in yet!" Sally called when I returned from my snowshoe outing. "Wouldn't you like to go snowshoeing for just a little while longer?" she asked sweetly through a crack in the door.

"No, I think I'll come in and sit by the warm fire for the next few days," I teased.

By Christmas eve we had finished our secret projects and we began a great baking spree with the extra supplies Ron had flown in. I made cookie cutters in the shape of a star, a Christmas tree, and a snowman from an extra piece of aluminum. We baked sugar cookies and decorated them with carob chips, raisins and nuts, then made mince tarts with the mince friends had sent in. All the various aromas of our baking melded into one delightful Christmasy fragrance which filled the cabin.

I had no trouble getting out of bed on Christmas morning. In fact, I was up first and even lit the fire.

"Merry Christmas, hurry up and get out of bed!" I called impatiently to Sally.

The cabin was especially cheerful: colourful decorations adorned the walls, felt Pak boot liners hung on the clothesline as our Christmas stockings, and presents were scattered under the gaily decorated Christmas tree.

My parents had sent us a box labelled, "Open me first." Inside the package was a bonanza of gifts—cashews, gum, toffees, lifesavers, chocolate bars, and small games and puzzles.

"Mom and Dad certainly knew what we would be craving after months in the bush!" I exclaimed happily, popping a candy into my mouth.

Next we opened a brightly-wrapped, three-foot cylinder, also from my parents.

"I bet it's a calendar!" Sally said as we pulled a paper out of the wrapper. We unrolled the paper and let out a simultaneous groan.... Somewhere my parents had found a two-by-three-foot poster of a chocolate sundae, illustrated in full colour detail down to the last mouthwatering drip of chocolate.

"How could they!" I laughed.

Then we selected a small box labelled, "Do not open until Christmas," which we had received from Sally's sister in the summer. Despite our many moments of weakness in the last months, the wrapper was still intact. Inside was a wonderful surprise package full of carefully-chosen and individually-wrapped presents, which included scented English soaps, Swiss soup-cubes, German coffee, Chinese herbal tea, Japanese soup mix, candy bars from Holland, and many other special food packages. After our simple fare of the last seven months, our eyes almost popped out at the sight of this array of international delicacies.

Our gifts to each other included a hand-carved wooden spoon, a candle holder, a coathook, and a carved wooden bowl. I watched Sally's eyes light up when she opened a most extravagant gift from me—an envelope of coupons which included two that read, "This coupon good for one early-morning firelighting."

We gorged ourselves on the special treats, washing mince tarts down with the English tea. By the afternoon, the tantalizing aroma of roast moose drifted through the cabin as our Christmas supper cooked in a cast-iron pot on top of the stove. We set the table with special attention: napkin rings made from hand-painted toilet paper rolls, new hankies for napkins and a centrepiece of a candle in a small can surrounded by spruce branches.

Our wilderness Christmas dinner was certainly unique. Our plates were loaded with roast moose, gravy poured over instant mashed potatoes, a cooked selection of dried vegetables, and bannock biscuits. Dinner was accompanied by a few treats that we had packed specially for the occasion: canned cranberry sauce, fruit cake, and a tiny airline bottle of rum to add to an eggnog of powdered milk and powdered eggs.

After supper we sang Christmas carols, but soon ran out of songs whose words we could remember. We tried our small A.M. radio, but the reception was poor and we could hardly hear the songs.

"Let's try hooking the radio up to the big aerial," Sally suggested. "Maybe the reception will be better."

"It won't work. It's a different kind of antenna," I stated, but Sally insisted that we try anyway. I ran a length of wire from the single-sideband radio antenna to the other radio's aerial, then turned it on. Much to my amazement (and Sally's satisfaction) it worked! We enjoyed a musical rendition of *Silent Night*, but when a deep voice came over the speaker, we couldn't understand a word of what the commentator said.

"Sounds like Russian to me!" Sally laughed. "But what the heck, the tune sounded familiar."

I turned the dial and the next voice that came over the small speaker sounded Chinese, although that station also featured familiar-sounding carols. I finally tuned in an Edmonton station. We groaned and drooled through a dialogue that went into great detail about Christmas in the city—Mandarin oranges wrapped in crinkly paper, hot turkey with all the trimmings, steaming plum pudding, mistletoe, and stockings hung by the chimney with care.

We sang along with the carols until we were hoarse, and finished off the rum eggnog and mince tarts. Then we went for a moonlit snowshoe trek to wear off the effects of too much supper.

The moon was almost full, and snow crystals thrown up by our snowshoes sparkled like tinsel in the silver light. Our breath swirled around us like silk scarves as we sang carols. At the end of one song we heard a wolf howl softly from deep in the forest. Sally imitated the call and the wolf responded with a low, sonorous howl that sounded more beautiful than any Christmas carol. We listened intently as the *Owoo-oo-oo* of the wolf echoed in the still night.

I held Sally close as we looked at the peaceful scene around us. No Christmas trees could equal those decorated by frosted crystals of snow. Stars flashed white, blue and red in the sky like a thousand Christmas lights above us, and our small cabin looked like a scene from a Christmas card. A thin white plume of smoke drifted straight up from the chimney, a candle glowed in the front window, and soft lines of snow swept around the cabin.

It had been a simple Christmas deep in the wilderness; one that seemed to represent Christmas as it should be—a quiet celebration on a peaceful night.

On Boxing Day we stuck the decorated tree into a snow-bank and waited expectantly for our furred and feathered friends to visit. It wasn't long before the Canada jays, pine grosbeaks, and chickadees chirped and flitted from branch to branch, feasting upon granola and popcorn. Soon, a squirrel came by, and the Canada jays and squirrel took turns tugging at the apple rings tied to the branches. But the squirrel quickly left when our friend the pine marten crept towards the tree. The marten was severely scolded by the Canada jays, and his efforts at chasing them were amusing but to little avail. The jays would taunt him, then fly away just before he could reach them.

The pine marten took his time investigating the tree, then stepped up and swung a paw at an aluminum-foil decoration. He pulled down a toilet-paper-roll ornament and played with it in the snow, then wrestled an apple ring

Wilderness Christmas

New Year's Eve

The cabin in winter

from the tree and ran into the forest with his prize. As soon as the marten left, the Canada jays returned and continued their squawking and squabbling.

"I think I'm going to enjoy the feeder tree as much as the animals do," Sally said as we watched the continuing antics of our visitors.

Our New Year's Eve festivities were also rather different than any we had ever before experienced. To start the fun we popped a batch of popcorn, unwrapped our monthly ration of one Mars Bar, and opened the half-bottle of champagne which Ron had brought in. One of the Christmas presents I had given Sally was a small package of New Year's party favours with whistles, kazoos, party hats, and balloons which I had packed eight months earlier. We put on the hats and our dancing boots and prepared to party, with music from our small radio.

We tuned the radio to an Alberta station and danced to a few faint songs. Just as we were getting ready to sing Auld Lang Syne, the reception faded.

"Oh no!" Sally said, "we'll miss the countdown."

"If we're lucky we can catch it on a B.C. station," I said. "They're in a time zone an hour later."

We turned the radio off to save the batteries, then waited for another forty-five minutes before turning the dial to CBC British Columbia. Then, for ten minutes, Sally and I had as wild a New Year's Eve party as two people could possibly have in a small cabin by the light of a kerosene lantern; we danced to music that faded in and out, ate the last of our popcorn, and drank thawed champagne.

At about five minutes before midnight the reception faded again.

"I don't believe it," I groaned.

Frantically, we tightened the antenna wire and retuned the radio. Then, just in time for the countdown, the sound came back. With party hats on, whistles ready, and pens poised over balloons, we counted down with the radio.

"Three ... two ... one.... Midnight! *Bang! Tweet! Yeehaw! Happy New Year!*" We drank toasts to the new year, and to our wilderness life, then finally went to bed —exhausted, happy, and slightly tipsy.

150

CHAPTER 17

Fifty Below!

I scraped a circle of thick frost from the front window and peered at the thermometer outside our cabin. In the dim morning light I could barely read the thin red line which hovered near the bottom of the scale.

"I think it reads fifty below!" I reported to Sally with disbelief. "I'm going outside to have a closer look."

"Hey, how about lighting the fire first?" Sally's muffled voice urged from deep within the down sleeping bag.

Sally had a good point—a skim of ice over the water bucket indicated that it was below freezing inside the cabin. The cabin logs had boomed loudly throughout the night, and a thick layer of frost and ice coated the door and windows. Frost crystals also lined the uppermost wall logs where they met the roof.

I lit the fire and filled the stove with dry wood. Then I bundled up in insulated overpants, parka, and Pak boots and went outside to investigate. We had a special thermometer which registered the lowest temperature each night, and I was curious to see how cold it had been.

As I opened the hand-hewn front door, a thick cloud of

cold mist billowed in along the floor.

"Close the door!" Sally exclaimed, still in bed. I pulled the door closed and frost tumbled down from the ledge above the door, showering me with delicate crystals.

Every bush and tree was dressed in a coat of fleecy white, and huge flakes of hoarfrost lay scattered across the snow. The air was so still that smoke from the cabin's stovepipe rose in a pencil-straight line to the frigid blue sky. My breath hung suspended in the air, and within moments, my bushy beard was encrusted by a thick layer of frost. Breathing the icy air was difficult; with each shallow breath, my nostrils burned and my chest tightened.

I checked the low-registering thermometer more closely, and saw that it had dropped to minus fifty-two overnight. The intense cold had brought with it an intense silence. The soft hush of early winter had been replaced by a clear, throbbing stillness, only occasionally broken by the thunder of a tree freezing. Chickadees had ceased their singing and moved sluggishly. Canada jays, which would normally have greeted my approach with an excited chattering and flapping of wings, now huddled miserably on their perches, puffed up like soft grey feather balls to keep warm. At first glance, it was hard to tell which end was which!

January was a season of rest in the north. The smooth covering of snow was untracked by recent marten, mice, or squirrel prints. Our furred and feathered friends had settled into their hollows and dens to wait for milder weather.

Like our animal neighbours, we spent most of our time indoors during this extremely cold weather. Tending the fire had become a full-time job; even though we wore thick pile pants and wool sweaters in the cabin, we had to stack wood in the stove every hour just to remain comfortable. Beyond the reach of the fire our cabin was cold. As in the days when families had gathered around the cheery warmth of the kitchen cookstove, our woodburning stove became the centre of the household.

To maintain a constant supply of firewood we had to make frequent forays to the woodpile. Although we bundled up warmly, our lungs burned and the frigid air stung our noses and cheeks. We had to work slowly to keep from inhaling the icy air too deeply. After only a few moments, our cheeks glowed rosy-red, and our eyebrows and eyelashes became white with hoarfrost.

Sally and I took turns splitting the wood, each working for fifteen minutes before warming up again inside the cabin. The woodpile was dwindling quickly, but it looked as though we would have enough to last through the winter.

"I'm glad we cut lots of firewood last fall," Sally mentioned one morning as she carried an armload of wood into the cabin. "I'd hate to be out in this weather dragging logs through the snow!"

Fetching water had also become a lengthy chore. Even though we insulated the water hole with a cover of spruce boughs and snow, it still froze to a depth of six or seven inches each night. We chopped through the ice by hacking away with the pointed, fifteen-pound peavy until the ice cracked. During this cold spell, it took twenty minutes just to chop through the ice and the buckets of water often froze over before we reached the cabin.

One morning while I was chopping through the ice, the peavy slipped out of my hands and plunged into the near-freezing water. I widened the hole with an axe and peered into the dark water. Fortunately, the peavy had stuck upright in the sandy bottom.

I rolled up a sleeve, took a deep breath and plunged my arm in. By stretching until my shoulder dipped into the icy water, I could just reach the peavy, but I couldn't get a grip on the slippery handle. I ran back to the cabin to thaw out and think of another strategy.

"What happened to YOU?" Sally asked as I stumbled into the cabin and over to the warm stove.

"Dropped the peavy . . . couldn't get it . . . too slippery," I mumbled unhappily.

"How about using a rubber glove to get a grip on the handle?" Sally suggested.

"Good idea! Why don't you try it?" I replied, shivering at the thought of plunging my arm into the water hole again.

"No way! You dropped it—you retrieve it!"

A few minutes later I returned to the cabin, waving my prize of the ice-sheathed peavy. I decided that once it had thawed, I would tie a rope around the handle so I wouldn't lose it again.

After our chores were done, we usually spent the rest of the day around the cabin and we became totally absorbed in novels, indoor projects or writing. Cabin relations became somewhat strained one afternoon as I read a humourous book, bursting into laughter every few minutes, while Sally read *Les Miserables* with tears in her eyes.

"I can't stand this! Why do you have to laugh out loud while I'm trying to read?" Sally complained.

"Because my book is funny," I giggled.

Sally glowered at me from behind her book.

"I think I'll go snowshoeing for a while," I said. This was our way of avoiding serious conflicts which could have developed between us, living as we did in such confined quarters. I don't think any two people could survive a winter cooped up in a small cabin without some time alone. Sally and I had found that we each needed space for mental and physical privacy. After a short outing we would return, happy to see each other again and eager to share our experiences.

I pulled on layers of clothing for the cold weather, starting with woollen long johns, heavy wool pants, bulky, insulated overpants, and felt-lined Pak boots. Then I dressed in a long-sleeved wool undershirt, a thick wool shirt, pile sweater, and a heavy down-filled parka. To top off my winter wardrobe I wore a pile cowl, wool toque, and a neoprene face mask so that no part of my face was exposed to the cold. On my hands were wool gloves, then pile-lined overmitts. When I was finished dressing, I looked and felt like an overstuffed teddy bear!

"I'm heading through the forest behind the cabin," I said, my voice muffled by the face mask. "I'll be back in an hour or so." For safety, we would tell each other where we were headed and would stick to a pre-planned route and return time.

Time alone in the silence of the forest was especially enjoyable. I became lost in my thoughts and let my mind wander to a book I had read, or to a warmer climate. Sometimes I would just stand among the tall, snow-laden trees and savour the freedom of the quiet forest.

On that afternoon the muffled shuffle of my snowshoes was the only sound in the forest. As I stopped to listen, the deep snow seemed to have absorbed every noise. I was startled by the dull thud of an axe on frost-hardened pine; in the clear still air I could hear Sally splitting firewood at the cabin a mile away. When the white silence of the woods was broken by a noise, it seemed even louder and more startling than usual.

I continued through the forest and crossed a line of caribou tracks leading up the mountain. During the cold, still weather, frigid air settled into the valleys, and the caribou must have been moving up the mountain where the temperature was slightly warmer. I followed the tracks and found an area of packed down snow where they had rested: seven distinct impressions of bodies and legs were clearly outlined in the soft snow.

Further along on a steep slope I saw where the caribou had scraped away snow with their hooves to expose moss and lichen to eat. I wanted to keep following the tracks with the hope of seeing caribou but it was after two o'clock and time to turn around; we never saw the sun, and the dull shadowless light of winter only lasted from ten until three.

When I arrived back at the cabin, Sally greeted me with laughter.

"You look hilarious!" she exclaimed, and brought me the small compass mirror.

I did look rather funny with huge, frosty eyebrows, long, icy eyelashes and half an inch of hoarfrost on my toque. White crystals laced my face mask and a thick layer of white rime coated my jacket collar, adding to the spectacle.

Although we had thought that the short days and cold weather of midwinter would keep us cabin bound, we were able to go snowshoeing almost every day. Sally became more restless in the cabin than I did, but we both found a daily outing necessary to keep away "cabin fever."

"Let's go to the Tucho River—I could use some exercise," Sally suggested one morning when the temperature hovered around forty below.

Sally and I took turns breaking trail through the deep snow in the forest, slowly lifting one snowshoe in front of the other. We became dressed from head to toe in white as our snowshoes kicked up fluffy snow. Every few minutes we wiped the back of a mitt across our frosty eyelashes to keep

155

them from freezing together when we blinked.

We snowshoed in silence, saving our conversation for back at the cabin. It was a special pleasure to listen, to look, and to be lost in our own thoughts with no outside interruption. Occasionally, one of us would stop and point out something of interest. Then we would continue quietly through the forest.

As we snowshoed along the river we heard a faint ringing bird song from the direction of the rapids. We were surprised to hear any birds singing in this frigid weather. We were even more surprised to see plump grey dippers splashing and swimming in the small area of open water at the rapids, seemingly oblivious to the cold. Another dipper stood on the snow doing a bobbing dance and whistled a merry musical song that echoed through the narrow valley. I wondered how these small birds could survive in the cold water, until we noticed a dipper primping and preening by picking up oil from the gland above its tail, then running its beak over each and every feather. The small bird then fluffed up its feathers and gave its tail such a hard shake it made us laugh.

After standing at the river for a few minutes, we felt the icy air seeping through our clothes. We drank a mug of sweetened tea from our thermos to ward off the cold, then headed back to the warmth of our cabin. Snowshoeing in the cold weather burned up a lot of energy, and we arrived back at the cabin tired after only two hours outdoors.

The spell of extremely cold weather lasted for almost three weeks. It was so cold that kersosene stored outside turned to a thick syrupy liquid, and we had to bring the axes inside to warm so they wouldn't shatter when we used them. The cabin logs boomed so often we thought the cabin would collapse around us. Trees constantly thundered in the forest, and ice cracked and boomed on the lake.

The icy grip of winter began to ease by late January. Although temperatures still remained far below freezing, the days of forty-five below zero weather were over. Birds and animals became more active, and we were pleased to have the martens, squirrels, jays and chickadees around the cabin again.

Sally and I were able to go on longer snowshoe trips as

Dressed for winter

Fifty below!

A quiet snowshoe trip

the weather warmed to a mere twenty below zero. One morning as we left the cabin we saw two black objects moving slowly along the south shore of the lake. We returned to the cabin for binoculars, then watched a cow moose and a calf struggling through the deep snow. We grabbed the camera, telephoto lens and tripod and set off across the lake on snowshoes.

It was difficult to move unnoticed across the lake, but we crept very slowly, one behind the other, and approached the pair from downwind. We were a thousand yards away when our movements caught the cow's attention.

The cow moose stood perfectly still, facing us for many minutes while the young calf nuzzled and nudged her impatiently. I moved closer, then set up the camera and tripod. As I focused the telephoto lens, the camera viewfinder was filled with the magnified image of nine hundred pounds of angry moose. I was so startled at the sight of the huge brown animal with hackles raised, and clouds of vapour billowing from flared nostrils, that I almost forgot to take the picture!

After I had taken a few photographs, the cow moose spun around and ploughed away from us through the deep snow, lifting her front legs very high like a trotter. I could see only the head and shoulders of the small calf as it struggled through the deep trough left in the snow by the cow. We worried for a moment that the mother would keep going without the calf as the little one lagged further and further behind, but the cow soon stopped and waited for the calf to catch up. After a quick nuzzle of reassurance, the mother and offspring continued together into the safety of the forest.

Photography at minus twenty Fahrenheit involved certain complications and challenges. Batteries didn't function well at cold temperatures, film became brittle and had to be rewound slowly, and cold metal could freeze to exposed skin. I kept the camera and lenses in an insulated bag to keep them warm, and sometimes used a small handwarmer to keep the camera equipment (and me!) from becoming too cold. Extra batteries in a shirt pocket were warm and ready to put in the camera if the others became too lethargic.

The expression, "with his eye glued to the camera," could become reality if I didn't wipe my frosted eyelashes before looking through the viewfinder. I didn't dare breathe with the camera near my face as the viewfinder and lens would instantly have been covered with a layer of frost. Even handling lenses with bare hands would frost the glass up, so I wore thin nylon gloves under my mitts for handling the camera.

With these simple precautions, the cameras functioned well, even down to minus thirty-five degrees. I decided that I didn't really want to be out taking pictures in weather colder than that!

Winter photography was worth the extra effort. The few animals and birds that had remained through the winter were rewarding subjects and the air was crystal-clear. Sharp white mountains were etched against a backdrop of blue sky. It was a season of subtle, soft colours, simple forms blanketed in white, and restful, snow-swept landscapes.

As January ended the days became longer and slightly warmer. We had made it through the roughest season. Sally and I had been warned about the "cruel northern winters," and "savage, bitter cold," and had faced the season with some apprehension. But with the worst of winter over, we found that our fears had been unfounded. Our firewood had held out, the cabin was cozy, and life had been rugged but rewarding. There had been time alone for reflective thought, and time together reading, writing, and sharing our innermost feelings.

CHAPTER 18

Late Winter

Just when Sally and I thought the worst of winter was over, we became snowed-in. Warmer weather during early February brought snowstorms raging through the valley, transforming the world outside our cabin into a whirlpool of swirling snow. Deep, soft snow filled in our footpaths around the cabin, making it impossible to go outdoors without snowshoes—even just to the outhouse!

Snowshoeing to the lake to fetch water was like entering a white void—no sight, no sound, and no sense of direction. We couldn't see further than our snowshoes, and our tracks were obliterated by drifting snow before we returned with our buckets of water. Every other sound was lost in the constant, eerie swishing of the snowstorm, and our voices seemed distant as they were whisked away by the wind.

"Well, at least it's better than fifty below," Sally shouted.

"I don't know about that," I hollered back. "At fifty below we didn't have to shovel snowdrifts from the door just to get into the cabin!"

We were isolated from the outside world more than ever

before. It would have been impossible to travel more than a few miles a day in the deep untracked snow; even wearing snowshoes, we sank up to our knees.

Although snowshoeing was difficult, we went on short outings during lulls in the storm. The forest was a fairyland setting of weird forms and figures, gargoyles and goblins, all carved by the wind. Mounds of snow weighted down trees and looked like white shawls around the shoulders of bent old women. Stumps were transformed into huge toadstools and our cabin seemed to be a fable cottage, with snow curling from the eaves, crescent-shaped snowdrifts snuggling up against the the cabin corners, and frost painting the window panes.

The storm finally eased after two weeks and three feet of snow. But it took another week, while we waited impatiently around the cabin, for the soft snow to settle. Finally we were able to enjoy the mobility of skis again, instead of having to slog along on our awkward snowshoes.

By early March, the sun arced higher in the sky each day, first peeking over Skyline Ridge, then cresting the ridge and flooding the land with brilliant light. On the first day of direct sunlight Sally and I rushed outside the cabin to welcome the return of the sun! We stood like sun-worshippers in the golden rays which shone on sparkling snow for five short but glorious minutes.

It had been more than three months since the sun had disappeared behind the southern ridge. The dull winter days inside our cabin had infected us with a mild case of cabin fever. During the last two months we had been able to go only on short outings, and we were becoming irritable. It wasn't until we found ourselves arguing over small things that we realized we had to do something about it.

"You know what would be really good for us?" Sally asked thoughtfully. "A ski trip towards the Rainbow lakes. Nothing will make our small cabin look better than spending a few nights camping in the snow!"

I looked at her sideways. The Rainbow lakes were nearly thirty miles northwest of us. It would take at least four days to ski there and back . . . if a blizzard didn't dump more snow. On the other hand, I realized the outing would be just the cure for our cabin fever.

"Okay," I said finally. "You're on!"

Within minutes, the cabin was a clutter of backpacks, clothes, sleeping bags, camp pots, and tent as we began our preparations for the ski trip. I looked at the pile of winter camping gear, extra clothing and fuel, and ski waxes and wondered aloud how everything would fit in our packs. We tried to think of ways to trim the weight of our packs, but all the equipment was essential; even the extra food was necessary in case we got caught in a snowstorm.

"What about leaving out the heavy arctic liners for our sleeping bags?" Sally suggested. "It hasn't gone below minus five for the last week."

"Sure, that will trim a couple of pounds," I agreed. "Just hope the temperature doesn't get much colder."

The next morning, we woke to clearing skies and the promise of sunny scenery later in the day. We quickly finished packing then dragged our heavy packs out the door.

I was strong enough to heave my heavy pack on with one motion, but Sally had developed a rather unique way of putting hers on. She refused any help, feeling that helping a lady on with her coat or pack was out of place in the wilds. I watched as she placed the pack in front of her, then took a deep breath.

"Umph!" Sally groaned as she hoisted the pack onto a bent knee and balanced it on her upper leg, then paused for a moment to catch her breath.

"Arrgh!" she shouted, and swung the pack onto her back, slipping her left arm through a shoulder strap. But the pack kept going and pulled her into the snow. Then, and only then, would she let me help.

We took turns breaking trail, as it was much easier to follow someone else's ski tracks than to take the lead in the deep, untracked snow. I led for twenty or thirty minutes and when my thigh muscles complained of the difficult work, I stepped aside to let Sally take her turn. We followed frozen waterways whenever we could; skiing on the wind-packed lakes and rivers was easier than in the woods, where soft snow and drifts made travel exhausting.

By late morning we were in terrain we had never skied before. Ahead lay new valleys and mountain peaks.

"Just think, we're probably the first people ever to explore this valley," Sally mused as we trekked across a meadow.

"Well, even if we're not the first people to explore here, I'm sure no one has ever skied here before," I replied.

As we swung into the Rainbow River valley, the scenery changed dramatically. The winding river was bordered by terraces and benches at different levels, and low alluvial ridges lay in parallel lines in the broad open valley, showing the history of the river. Long ago a glacier had carved the valley floor into a U shape, leaving foothills rising gradually to the mountains.

The familiar mountains around Hottah Lake grew small as new ranges unfolded before us. To the west were the enormous white summits of the Stikine range. The few mountains that had names on our map told of tall majestic peaks. King Mountain, Spike Mountain, and Sharktooth Mountain were apt names for towering pinnacles and obelisk peaks that reached over seven thousand feet skyward.

Just when our packs began to feel as though they weighed a hundred pounds, we found an ideal camping spot. It was sheltered by trees, safe from avalanche danger, and, best of all, an open crack in the ice of the river meant we wouldn't have to use our valuable fuel to melt snow for water.

Setting up camp in winter was quite different from setting up camp in the summer. First, we packed down an area in the snow with our skis and then waited fifteen minutes for the snow to harden before setting up our small nylon tent. While I went for water, Sally dug a shallow pit in front of the tent. Then she built a windbreak for the stove while I unpacked sleeping pads and bags.

With a little coaxing, the small Optimus stove roared to life, and soon we were preparing a concoction of freeze-dried stew which we affectionately called "mush." Meals were not a leisurely affair when winter camping—we had to eat supper quickly before the food froze in the pot, and it was a challenge to hold spoons while wearing thick mitts. We sat bundled up in all our clothing and devoured supper as twilight faded to dusk.

Sally and I climbed into the tent and watched the last

golden rays of sunlight splash across the valley floor. The tent door framed a wilderness portrait, with the ice-covered Rainbow River gracefully curving through the foreground. Tall peaks were outlined against the pale, amber sky, and a few scattered clouds reflected the sun's last rays.

We nestled down into the warmth of our sleeping bags, sharing them with rather odd bedfellows. Socks and mitts lay between the sleeping bag and pad to dry overnight, and the stove pump, butane lighter and my contact lenses were inside the foot of my sleeping bag where they would not freeze. A water bottle filled with hot water was a pleasant source of warmth, and in the morning would provide unfrozen water for breakfast.

I woke in the night to the spine-tingling howl of wolves somewhere near our camp.

"Sally," I whispered, nudging her through the sleeping bags.

"I hear them," she replied. "They sound so close . . . like they're right beside the tent. I know wolves don't attack people, but it's hard not to think of mythical wolves with flaming eyes and flashing fangs when they're all around us!"

The howls became louder until we could clearly hear each wolf through the thin nylon walls of our tent. Five distinct voices joined in a harmony of howling which reverberated in the still night air. The wolves continued their howling for almost an hour before their voices faded as the pack moved away.

When the first light of morning illuminated the valley, Sally and I rubbed the sleep from our eyes. We wriggled into our clothes while we lay in our narrow sleeping bags, then clambered outside. We had slept well, and were eager to push on towards the Rainbow lakes.

By mid afternoon we arrived at the first lake and set up camp on a point of land at the north end. The lake was about four miles long by one mile wide, with a number of dark, treed islands thrusting up from its flat white surface.

"Look over there," I said, pointing across the lake. "Caribou . . . or something. Let's go have a look."

"Looks like boulders to me," Sally commented. "It will seem awful silly if we ski all the way across just to see some rocks."

"It will be even more silly if we don't go and there ARE animals over there," I replied, confident that animals, and not rocks, were across the lake.

As we skied closer the objects became recognizable—a herd of thirteen caribou was resting at the edge of the lake. I slowly took off my pack and pulled out the camera and telephoto lens. The lighting for photography was perfect: low sun cast a warm, yellow light on the caribou, and glistened on their chestnut-brown fur. The caribou's fur was accented by white collars and silver-white underbodies, rumps and legs. Large, majestic antlers on the males and females curved high over their shoulders and were outlined dramatically against the snow.

It wasn't often when photographing wildlife that I had plenty of time to compose a picture. Usually, the animals moved too quickly or the sun was in the wrong place, making them difficult to photograph. But everything was right that afternoon: the caribou even stood patiently in a long line, as if posing for a group portrait.

As I continued to take pictures, the caribou slowly turned in unison and trotted away. Then, a wildlife photographer's dream came true. They stopped and came back towards us for a second look. I had heard of caribou curiosity, but this was amazing! We stared. They stared. We moved back. They moved forward. I whistled a ragtime tune and they came even closer, then trotted away, only to return again for another look. Sally and I sang and danced for our appreciative audience until they became bored by our antics and wandered away.

Caribou had been one of the animals at the top of our "want list" to photograph, and we headed back to our tent elated at having seen and photographed this magnificent animal.

That evening was cold and clear. We sensed that the temperature was dropping and gathered wood for a small campfire. Sally and I sat around the warmth of the fire until late in the evening, then took our plastic bottles of hot water to bed.

"Hope it doesn't get much colder!" I repeated each time we woke during the cold night. I reminded Sally that it had been her idea to leave the sleeping bag liners behind. Never

Winter camp

Caribou

Exploring new country

again! We shook, shivered, and shuddered as the temperature plunged to minus twenty degrees. We woke repeatedly through the night, tossing and turning, and adding more clothing in an effort to keep warm. When daylight finally came I didn't feel as though I had slept a wink. It was the kind of morning when a person feels like crawling down into the sleeping bag and staying there. Under other circumstances I might have seen beauty in the pattern of frost crystals that coated the walls of our tent and hung down in lacy ribbons from the zipper. At other times I might have appreciated the aesthetic appeal of the frost crystals which showered down upon us when we bumped the tent walls. Even the delicate designs of thick hoarfrost on my sleeping bag might have looked pleasing to the eye from a warmer vantage.

Sally's journal entry reflected what she felt was the worst about our cold night: "I lay in my sleeping bag until my bladder was almost bursting. How horrible to have to climb from my sleeping bag and out into the cold night air!"

We lay shivering in our sleeping bags until the valley was warmed by the touch of the rising sun. First priority was hot tea and some breakfast. Then we started to pack up camp.

"This is not everybody's idea of a good time," Sally said, shivering as we stuffed frosty sleeping bags into frigid stuff sacks with our near-frozen fingers.

"Not mine either," I said, and winked, nearly freezing my eyelashes closed. "Did I ever tell you how much I like winter camping?"

"Don't—I think I can guess," Sally replied.

Our hands were so cold that it took a long time to pack up camp. Sally continued to stuff a frosted sleeping bag into a small nylon sack while I warmed her gloves and overmitts by blowing into them. When her fingers became numb with cold, I took my turn packing.

Our Ensolite foam pads cracked as we tried to roll them up, breakfast froze in the pot before we could finish it, and my contact lenses were frozen in their salt solution—even though they had been in my sleeping bag! All in all, it was a.... Well, let's just say it was a memorable experience.

We decided to try skiing the entire thirty miles home in one day—anything to avoid spending another night out.

167

With our ski tracks to follow, and no route-finding to slow us down, our return trip was faster, but it was a physical and mental challenge to push ourselves when our muscles began to ache and our feet grew numb from cold. Lunch was just a quick stop, then we pushed on, knowing that if we had to spend the night out we would be even more miserable.

By the time we had skied twenty miles we were plodding along, oblivious to our sore backs, tired legs, and to our surroundings. We focused on the ski tracks ahead of us, concentrating on pushing one ski ahead of the other. Left, right, left, right. Suddenly, a loud whirr of wings startled us out of our trance as six ptarmigans flew up, cackling loudly.

"Jeez, I almost had a heart attack!" I yelled.

"Don't you dare, I've got enough to carry," Sally retorted.

We finally arrived at Hottah Lake after eight long hours of skiing. It took another hour to ski the two miles across the lake, and it seemed like an eternity. A Hilton hotel couldn't have looked more inviting than our small rustic log cabin as we skied into our bay in semi-darkness. Sally skied to the edge of the lake, and dropped her pack into the snow.

"I'll get it later," she mumbled, and stumbled up the path to the cabin.

All I could think of was warmth when we finally reached the cabin, but even the cabin was cold. Water on the stove had frozen and the windows were frosted from top to bottom. I lit the fire, then we sat on the edge of the bed, neither talking nor moving, while the fire warmed the cabin and supper cooked on the stove.

My muscles felt as if I had completed a marathon. We had skied thirty rugged miles in nine hours, carrying thirty-five-pound packs on our backs. Exhaustion swept over me, but I also had the satisfaction of knowing we had pushed ourselves to the limit of our endurance.

For the next few days we were quite happy to stay at home. In fact, we had little energy to do anything but eat and rest. My journal entry for March the fourth summed up our feelings: "Day of rest. Unpacking, drying, and mending equipment, but no skiing! Our cabin fever is cured. For the time being I am quite content to be warm, full, and to sleep on a foam mattress instead of the snow."

CHAPTER 19

Kutcho Creek

How quickly the memory of that cold night and the other hardships of our ski trip faded! Six days later the trip didn't seem too bad, and after eight we remembered only the good parts—the scenery, the wolf serenade, the beautiful sunset of the first night, the curious caribou. After ten days we were talking of going on another trip.

"What's this pencil mark at Kutcho Creek?" Sally asked one evening as she looked over a map. "Didn't the old trapper say there was a summer prospecting camp there?"

We were still without radio communication and the sudden thought that an emergency radio might be at the camp brought me to my feet.

"Let me see," I said, leaning over Sally's shoulder. I was concerned that our parents would be worried about us. If by some chance there was a radio at the camp, we could let them know we were still O.K. and arrange to have some extra supplies flown in.

I measured the distance to Kutcho Creek. "Look, it's about ten inches from Hottah Lake. That's only fifty miles away. If we can ski through this valley . . . and if there is a camp, maybe it will have a radio. . . . "

"That's a lot of if's and maybe's," Sally interrupted. "But we could ski to Kutcho Creek to see what's there!

We waited for five days, hoping the weather would clear, then decided to head out, regardless. It was the third week of March, and as Sally said, "We might have to wait 'till summer for good weather. Let's just go!"

This trip would be a long haul. It would test our endurance, and route-finding skills more than ever before, but we looked forward to the challenge. It would take at least six days to ski to the camp and back—if it was even there. A snowstorm or poor skiing conditions could add several days to the trip.

We shouldered our packs early the next morning, and skied past Gray Lake, following the same route we had skied to the Rainbow lakes. By late afternoon we turned south and began skiing up a wide valley. We had a difficult route decision to make at that point: we could ski up through the forest and over a ridge to cut six miles off the route, or we could follow the river valley—the distance would be greater, but the route-finding and skiing would be easier.

"I think we should follow the river," I suggested. Years of experience had taught me that shortcuts often took longer. Our maps didn't always show thick forest, gulleys or other obstacles.

Caribou tracks led along the winding river—they too must have known from experience that the snow was firmer and less deep on the rivers. Even so, the caribou had a difficult time; their tracks were over a foot deep, and in some places wide troughs showed where the caribou had pushed through snow drifts with their chests.

By five o'clock we were ready to pitch camp. We had skied almost twenty miles, and felt tired, but content after a full day in the wild country that we loved. Sally and I quickly set up the tent and then cooked a supper which stuck to our ribs—and the camp pot.

"I'll do the dishes," I offered, picking up the pot and two spoons. I scrubbed the pot with a handful of coarse snow before the remnants of stew could freeze to the bottom, then filled the pot with water for hot chocolate.

"Only one problem with the one-pot system," Sally said,

taking a sip from her mug as we lay in the tent. "This hot chocolate has the distinct essence of stew!"

Daylight came just after seven the next morning. The mountain tops glowed with pale-orange light that slowly edged towards the valley, but the warm colours of sunrise were deceiving, and we crawled reluctantly out of our warm sleeping bags. By the time we had finished breakfast and packed up camp, the golden, morning sky had turned to a dull silver haze. Within an hour light snowflakes were drifting down, but we pushed on, hoping for only a light snowfall.

Later that morning, snow sifted steadily from the grey sky and visibility was poor in the flat, white light. I skied behind Sally, following the narrow tracks that her skis left in the snow. Only occasionally did I glance up to peer into the snowstorm.

Then, as we skied over a small rise, Sally dropped out of sight.

All I could see as I skied into the white void was Sally's ski pole waving below me. Carefully I moved closer. I peered over the edge of a four-foot bank and saw Sally lying face down in the snow, pinned by her heavy pack. She had skied over the bank and plunged straight down.

"Are you O.K.?" I yelled.

"I think so ... but I'm stuck!"

Sally couldn't reach her pack buckle or ski binding releases, making it impossible for her to move. As I dug her out, she described what had happened.

"Suddenly my skis dropped out from under me! I landed in the snow with one arm buried to the shoulder, and my pack pushing me into the snow. I was worried that I had broken a ski. Or worse, that you would follow my tracks and fall on top of me!"

We were in what is called "whiteout" weather. As the name implies, everything was lost in a white whirlpool which hid the mountains, forest and valley. The featureless sky and snow merged into an bleak landscape with no depth, no shadows, no past or future.

Needless to say, skiing in whiteout conditions was dangerous. Once shadows disappeared on the white landscape it was impossible to determine what was ahead of our skis—whether the slope went up, down, into a deep hollow, or was flat. We were fortunate that Sally had skied off only a four-foot bank, and not a twenty-foot precipice. To prevent further accidents, we decided to remain where we were and wait out the weather.

Huddled together in the middle of the whiteout, we felt small and vulnerable, dwarfed by the rage of the snowstorm. We had learned that nature was in control in the north; one can't rush a snowstorm or a cold night. The storm would continue, regardless of our actions.

There was nothing beyond our ski tips, no feeling of time; only emptiness in a white space, with phantom walls, floor and ceiling. We strained our eyes, looking for an image in the void, any image. How long would the whiteout last? Would we sit here for half an hour or overnight?

With nothing to look at or focus on, our thoughts turned inward. We sat quietly, wrapped in a space blanket for warmth, each absorbed in our own reflections. To keep myself from dwelling on the storm, I thought of warmer climates and summer days. It was a mental game I had learned to play at times like this: the swishing of the snow was not unlike the rhythm of waves on a beach; the space blanket around my shoulders became a beach towel.

After an hour, images began to reappear. Slowly, the dark spectral shapes of trees became visible. Mountains and valleys began to emerge from the emptiness as the landscape acquired shadows, depth and texture.

We skied for another hour and stopped when we found a sheltered campsite. Because it was still snowing we set up camp quickly, and settled into our sleeping bags earlier than usual.

The next morning we continued along the west side of the Kutcho valley. Willow bushes lay hidden under the snow and collapsed as we skied over them, making our progress slow and frustrating.

"Hell! This place is booby-trapped!" I swore as the snow gave way beneath me and I tumbled face first into the snow for the third time in a mile. Even Sally, who was following for awhile, was breaking through. With the burden of our heavy packs it was extremely difficult to dig ourselves out.

It was nearly time to stop for the night, when I spotted a

dark object in the distance that looked like a building. With renewed determination, if not energy, we decided to continue. We were tired and hungry, but thoughts of spending a night in a shelter instead of our cold tent lured us onward.

We skied towards the camp in the deepening mountain twilight, two bent figures slogging along, struggling to push one ski ahead of the other. By the time we reached the camp, about two hours later, we were just able to summon the energy to ski briskly up to a brown plywood cabin. There, we were greeted by a tall, bearded man in blue denim coveralls.

A real person! Sally and I stood tongue-tied, oblivious to our heavy packs. We had not seen another human being since Ron's Christmas visit, three months earlier. We certainly hadn't expected to find a person at this remote camp!

We stared at the towering man with his mass of black curly hair and huge bushy beard. Our surprise at seeing him at this remote camp must have equalled his surprise at seeing us ski to his door. I managed to utter a hello or something equally profound.

"Hi," he said, his face expanding into a friendly smile. "Come on in—you must have skied a long way!"

"About fifty miles . . . three days from Hottah Lake," I answered.

He shook his head in wonder. "Long way to visit your nearest neighbour!"

Over tea, then supper, we learned that our host, Don Weir, was the winter caretaker for this remote jade exploration camp. We were his first winter visitors in three years.

We quickly overcame our initial shyness. As we relaxed, our tongues untied and we talked about northern life, bush pilots, and our experiences in the wilderness. We found that Don certainly didn't have to ask why we were spending a winter in this remote and rugged country—he understood and shared our love of the outdoors, wildlife, and the north. We were as interested in Don's lifestyle as he was in ours, and although we were all a little awkward with words, we talked until one in the morning, when our voices finally faltered.

The next morning, Don showed us around the valley, pointing out the caribou herding and grazing areas and other sights. Although he extolled the virtues of snowshoes over skis, I'm sure I caught a glance of envy when Sally and I schussed down slopes that he had to snowshoe. As we travelled along a ridge behind the cabin, a red fox loped out of the trees. The fox was a graceful animal, and as it trotted, its bushy red tail with its snow-white tip hung loosely behind. Don gave a low whistle and the fox stopped, watched us for a few minutes, then continued into the forest. Don had as many interesting animal neighbours as we did. He told us of a rabbit that often followed him as he snowshoed the camp's small airstrip, and of his pet marten that would come into the cabin porch each evening for a bowl of milk. The red fox also frequented the camp, and one morning Don had looked up from reading to see the fox looking in the window at him, front paws on the sill and nose pressed against the glass.

When we returned from our outing Don offered to cook us supper. "How does steak and lobster sound?" he asked enticingly.

"I'll have my steak medium-well," I answered with a laugh, thinking Don was joking.

My eyes almost bugged out when he returned from his freezer with three steaks and a lobster in the shell! Don was well supplied with excellent food: no beans and bannock at his camp. Don had a seemingly unlimited food budget and told us with a chuckle that he had radio-telephoned his supplier one day for an air drop and asked them not to send in any more sirloin roasts. "My pine marten won't settle for anything less than sirloin tip," he had explained. Base personnel had been unsure whether to send in the supplies he requested or to bring him out because he had been in the bush too long!

"I have a supply flight coming in a couple of weeks," Don said. "Would you like the pilot to drop anything off at your camp?"

"That would be great—we could use more film," I replied enthusiastically.

On our second evening with Don, the weather conditions were suitable for radio communication and he offered to let us call out on his high-frequency radio. We were unfamiliar with the radio and doubted our ability to handle the seemingly complex task of talking to a radio-telephone operator.

Don understood the slightly abnormal behavior of two who have been in the bush for too long, and put the calls through for us. We waited nervously as Don pressed the call button.

"Watson Lake operator, go ahead radio," crackled over the small speaker.

"This is Jadex, how are you reading us, operator?"

"About two by five, radio," came the static-filled reply, indicating that she could hear us fairly well.

Don then asked the operator to connect us with Sally's parents in Montreal. It had been more than nine months since we had talked with them and we waited with butterflies in our stomachs as we heard the phone ring.

"Hello," a faint voice answered.

"Have you ever talked on a high-frequency radio before?" the operator asked.

"No, but I'll give it a try," we heard Sally's father reply.

"Go ahead, radio," the operator instructed.

"Hello—this is Sally!" Sally yelled into the small hand microphone.

"You're still alive! How are you? ... Where are you?" crackled over the speaker.

Sally's parents had tried unsuccessfully to reach us several times by radio, and were relieved to finally hear from us. We had an exciting five-minute call, during which many months of news was summarized. Then the reception faded.

Next, we called my parents in Nanaimo, B.C., and although conversation was difficult due to poor radio reception, we had a wonderful call. My Mom and Dad had the dubious honour of being our support crew, and we relied on them to arrange a supply drop of film and such much-needed but hard-to-acquire oddities as ski waxes, special camera batteries and other diverse items.

My parents also crammed months of news into the short call, and a comment from my mother reflected her thoughts of our adventure, "You guys are sure brave, or crazy, or both, to ski fifty miles to that camp! But then someone who is BUSHED will do almost anything for a different face and a meal!"

All three of us were grinning from ear to ear after the contact with our families.

"You're lucky," Don said. "I didn't want to tell you this, but that radio hasn't worked for the last week."

We had a wonderful visit with Don. For two days we shared the good-humoured camaraderie of the trail, and evenings of quiet conversation back at the cabin. When we talked of returning to Hottah Lake, Don told us of an old prospector and a trapper who lived in the next valley and suggested we visit them.

"They're as isolated as you, and would really enjoy some company," Don said.

We had heard stories about the "mad trapper" of Letaine Lake and were a little apprehensive about visiting, but Don assured us that the trapper was friendly—if a little eccentric.

"The only danger I can think of is from dysentery if he offers you supper," Don chuckled.

"Oh, one more thing ... ," he cautioned. "Just don't sneak up on him!"

CHAPTER 20

Mountain Men

Only a few, fleeting clouds punctuated the sky as we skied from Don's cabin the next morning. Don accompanied us for an hour, then pointed out a route up a long narrow pass that led to the next valley.

"Climb over this pass, then head south up the Letaine Valley to Paul and Andy's cabins. You'll find them at the edge of this lake," Don said, drawing a pencil line on our map. "I wish I could go with you!"

The day was already warm as Sally and I began the slow, steady climb towards the six-thousand-foot pass. By the time we were halfway up we had stripped down to T-shirts, and as we climbed higher our backs became drenched with perspiration. The route was quickly dubbed, "Perspiration Pass." Dripping sweat and the unrelenting glare of the sun stung our eyes as we struggled to the summit.

We crested the summit and looked down on a steep mountainside of huge cornices and forbidding windswept scree slopes. The first line of timber lay fifteen-hundred feet below us down a steep snowy incline.

"After you!" I offered as we stared down the mountainside. Don had told us that the slope was steep, but we hadn't realized that it would be far too difficult to ski. The only other possible routes were rocky and exposed; if we slipped, we would fall hundreds of feet down the jagged bluffs.

"How about traversing across to that gulley, then sliding down on our bums?" Sally suggested.

Deciding that we had no other option, we crossed over to the gulley, then strapped the skis to our packs and cautiously slid down the first eight hundred feet, in a spray of cold, wet snow.

When we considered the slope to be safe enough to ski, we buckled on our skis and pushed off . . . down, down, the snowy mountainside. Cautiously, we carved wide telemark turns through the deep snow: falling with a forty-pound pack would have done little for our ego or our vertebrae. We arrived at the bottom, with our leg muscles shaking from the exertion. Looking back up, we saw our flowing signatures carved in the white parchment of snow.

We continued down a narrow valley to Letaine Creek. Here, we turned south and followed the route Don had pencilled on our map. I looked around, trying to recognize our surroundings in the series of narrow lines on our topographic map. King Mountain dominated the western end of the Letaine Valley and smaller, but no less impressive, peaks crowned the northern and southern horizons.

It was late afternoon when we finally approached Paul's camp. We skied cautiously towards the low cabin, unsure of the kind of reception we would receive.

"Remember what Don said—don't sneak up on him," I reminded Sally. "Let's yell a hello from here."

Sally and I bellowed out a greeting, then waited for a response. As we skied closer, a small, hyperactive Scottish terrier announced our arrival by barking and jumping into the air. Finally, an authentic "mountain man" appeared at the cabin door.

"Ho there!" greeted the mountain man in a big, friendly voice. He strode over from the doorway, and before Sally could say anything he was helping her take her pack off.

The man behind the big voice was a small, wiry trapper named Paul Jensen. He had a quick, almost toothless, smile, a stubbly grey beard and intense, sparkling blue eyes. From

178

the wool toque perched on his head and the improvised scarf that was nothing more than an old pant leg tied around his neck, to the hand-made, caribou-hide boots he wore on his feet, he dressed the part of a mountain man. Thick woollen pants, suspenders, a grey, woollen undershirt, and a pair of thick socks which served as mittens, completed his unique attire.

"Come in, come in.... Coffee's on!" he said, animatedly waving us inside.

We had found that northern hospitality meant being invited in for coffee, supper, and to stay overnight before anyone even asked who you were or where you came from. It was an unwritten code of ethics that any traveller be made welcome, and we immediately felt at ease with our host's warm hospitality.

We entered the cabin through a door made from a large hollow tree trunk cut in half, then followed Paul's dark shadow down an eerie, unlit corridor lined with fox pelts, beaver skins and caribou hides. The hind quarter of a large animal swung menacingly as Paul brushed by it. My eyes adjusted to the dimness once Paul lit a flickering candle, and I gazed around the cabin. The walls were built from vertical logs nearly two feet thick, the floor was laid with flat stones, and small windows had been fashioned from glass jars cemented together with mortar.

Being a true mountain man, Paul lived with as few outside goods as possible. He made his own candles from animal fat, he built and strung his own snowshoes, and he had specially crafted a sled from moose hide to haul firewood. He had even roofed his cabin with hand-split shakes, giving it a rustic charm.

This was Paul's spruce castle, complete with a stone fireplace and large comfortable chairs of hollow logs upholstered with caribou hides. His cluttered kitchen table held the usual complement for a wilderness coffee break: a can of condensed milk with two knife holes punched in the top, a tin can for a sugar bowl, and another can sprouting knifes, forks and spoons.

A soot-black coffee pot bubbled away on the barrel stove. Paul wiped out two mugs with his shirttail and poured us each a mug of thick, black coffee with, as Paul said, "just a little whisky." After pottering about in various dark corners and crannies for several minutes, he proudly presented us with a piece of crusty bannock and a slab of dusty caribou jerky.

"The body needs food, liquid and a little alcohol after a hard workout," he explained cheerfully.

Sally eyed the food suspiciously, then glanced at me sideways, obviously remembering Don's warning about dysentery. I broke off a piece of bannock and quickly washed it down with a gulp of coffee, not wishing to offend our host. Sally sipped her coffee and nibbled the bannock cautiously.

"Have some jerky," Paul insisted. "Made it myself." He dusted a chunk of meat on his shirt and placed it beside Sally's coffee cup.

"Thanks," Sally replied weakly, "but I'm just thirsty right now." It was nearing suppertime, and when Paul offered to hack a piece of caribou meat off the dried carcass hanging in the hall, Sally quickly said that she would make some of our soup.

Paul was more than my match in garrulity and we found him to be both knowledgeable and opinionated about current affairs. In this open valley he was able to get good radio reception, and listened to the news each day on a small radio. Paul also did a great deal of reading. Except for an occasional supply flight, he rarely had any visitors, and he talked non-stop until late into the evening about everything from politics to packhorses and pelts. Even after we had bedded down on caribou-hide mattresses, he was still chatting.

"It's daylight in the swamp," Paul announced cheerfully the next morning as he rekindled the fire. The small windows of his cabin transmitted little light, so he lit sputtering candles and a hissing propane lamp.

The soup-encrusted cauldron was deemed fit to prepare oatmeal in after Paul had taken a quick swipe at it with a dishrag. The porridge was accompanied by pieces of dried caribou meat and gallons of black, black coffee. Sally looked at me and shrugged, then dished out a generous amount of canned milk and brown sugar onto her porridge. I could see her mustering her courage, but finally she tried a spoonful of the mush. Since she showed no immediate symptoms of an adverse reaction, I added a few lumps of brown sugar to my bowl and dug in.

"I like a breakfast that will stay with me all day!" Paul explained, waving a spoonful of oatmeal in the air for emphasis.

"I hope it will," Sally replied with a crooked smile.

After breakfast, Paul offered to take us on a guided tour of his valley. While we put on gaiters, light ski boots and cross-country skis, Paul strapped up his knee-length fur leggings with a length of rawhide, and donned a pair of old leather downhill ski boots and antique mountaineering skis. For traction, he slathered his skis with a mixture of spruce pitch and animal fat. With an old pair of ski goggles perched on his forehead and a wineskin slung over his shoulder, he led us down the valley, talking all the way. Like a tour-bus narrator, Paul pointed out beaver lodges, animal tracks, a caribou grazing-area, and mountain goat hills, while his tiny terrier bounded about us, and chased ptarmigan.

At sixty-six, Paul had a youthfulness in his stride and a twinkle in his eye that are lacking in many a city man half his age. He moved fluidly and gracefully on his skis, and when it came to downhill runs he was a real speed demon. Paul blasted straight down hills and jumps, grinning from ear to ear and whooping and hollering, with his energetic dog running after him.

We arrived back at the cabin famished, and having survived two meals we decided Paul's food was harmless enough. With our vote of confidence, Paul rustled up a caribou roast complete with onions, potatoes and carrots. He made gravy, carefully sifting in flour until it was, in his words, "just right—maybe perfect!" The meal looked large enough to feed a small army but Sally and I had regained our appetites and there was little left after second and third helpings.

The next morning we skied with Paul the two miles to his brother Andy's cabin, where we were greeted by a well-mannered dog. When Andy came to the door and quietly invited us inside for coffee we immediately sensed that he was the complete opposite of Paul. Andy was a soft-spoken old gentleman who kept an immaculate cabin, dressed well and was clean shaven, even though he lived in isolation.

His small, tidy plywood cabin had a propane stove, Plexiglass windows and an aluminum roof. Loaves of store-bought bread, rows of canned food, and a VHF radio showed that although Andy was as independent and isolated as Paul, he liked the refinements of civilization.

"They call me Chef Boy-ar-dee," he said, smiling when we noticed the long row of cans along the wall.

We told Andy of our cabin at Hottah Lake and shared stories of our ski trip to Kutcho Creek and over the pass. He was a good listener and liked to laugh, even though he confided, "I don't get much chance to laugh, living alone."

Andy was a quiet, sincere person who disliked trapping and made his living prospecting for jade. It was obvious that his views and Paul's conflicted, and that they seemed to thrive on goading each other.

"I got a fox this week!" Paul commented proudly.

"Would rather you'd let it live," Andy replied sharply.

While we talked, Paul offered to make coffee. He picked up the bright, clean, coffee percolator, disdainfully set the perking basket aside and threw in handful of grounds, camp-coffee style. When the coffee came to a boil, Andy looked over and wondered aloud why it wasn't perking.

"It'll be ready in a minute," Paul brusquely assured him. "I made it the proper way, without that new-fangled burpolater!"

Andy smiled at us and shrugged, "Now you know why our cabins are two miles apart!"

After a short, but fascinating visit, we reluctantly left the two brothers and started on our long ski trip home. Instead of trying to ski back the way we had come, over the steep mountain pass, we decided to travel around the mountain by following Letaine Creek.

Sally and I skied along the valley until we reached the junction with Kutcho Creek, where we stopped for the night. We came across our old ski tracks only an hour after breaking camp the next day, but unfortunately a herd of caribou had found them before us and had ruined our tracks by walking on them. The caribou had obviously liked travelling along the packed snow of our ski tracks because a long procession of hoof prints followed every bend and curve of our trail for many miles.

It began snowing lightly just as we stopped for the second night, and by the morning the tent was sagging under two inches of wet snow. But as we packed up camp, the sky cleared and the new snow made travelling fast and enjoyable. The caribou had left our old tracks, and the faint depression of ski tracks which still remained under the new snow led us back home.

By late afternoon we were approaching Gray Lake and familiar country. We were looking for a sheltered place to pitch camp when Sally noticed a full moon slowly rising over the mountains.

"Let's keep skiing to the cabin by moonlight," Sally suggested.

"Do you feel strong enough?" I asked, inspired by the thought of skiing home under a full moon, but worried that we were too tired.

"Sure," Sally replied energetically. "At this pace it should only take us another three or four hours."

We stopped for a quick supper, then continued skiing as the last rays of daylight dwindled to muted shades of blue. The change from daylight to darkness was very gradual. As the purple hues of alpenglow faded, the sky and snow seemed to merge, and our path was illuminated by the silver light of the full moon.

The evening seemed magical as we skied through the silver snow, with sparkling ice-crystals swirling from our ski tips. Although we could not see the route clearly, we felt our previous trail under our skis and could tell when we strayed off the tracks into deep snow. We recognized many features in the dull moonlight: the flat surface of Gray Lake, the uneven patches of willow swamps, and each familiar twist of the trail. In the distance, outlined against the night sky, we recognized the silhouettes of the mountains above Hottah Lake.

We continued along the Tucho River, listening to the faint murmur of water flowing beneath the ice. Then we glided across the windpacked surface of Hottah Lake, our skis like hickory wings beneath our feet. The black shape of our cabin, almost hidden under a blanket of snow, looked cozy and inviting as we skied into our bay.

After a second and more satisfying supper, we sat around

the warm stove and recalled the events and excitement of our trip. We had shared the hospitality and companionship of others who lived in remote wilderness, talked to our parents by radio, and skied further than we had ever ventured before—all because of a faint "X" that someone had drawn on our map!

CHAPTER 21

A Northern Spring

"Do you realize that, according to the calendar, spring began two weeks ago?" Sally said, as she crossed off the seventh of April.

The month of April was certainly not spring in the north country. Not with four feet of snow in the forest and four feet of ice on the lake. Snowshoes and skis were still an essential part of our travel and we often kept the stove burning all day just to keep our cabin warm.

Winter did show signs of easing though. Slowly, ever so slowly, nature was waking from its long winter slumber. We had already seen the first fluffy, grey pussy willow blossoms peeking through the snow. And each day the sun arced higher, flooding our valley with light from eight in the morning until seven o'clock in the evening.

But Sally and I had little time to dawdle over pussy willows and the other signs of spring. We had to pack a runway on the lake for the ski-plane which we expected to arrive within a week. Snowshoeing a landing strip fifty feet wide and a quarter-mile long was a monotonous task that took us almost three hours, but the snow had to be packed firmly enough to support the weight of the plane.

Only hours after we had finished the runway, it began snowing. By the next morning the runway was obliterated by snow. For the next four days, we snowshoed up and down the runway each morning. Each afternoon it snowed, burying the airstrip again.

On the morning of April fourteenth the weather cleared, and we wearily trod up and down the runway again. Around noon we heard the distant drone of a plane. Our supply flight! We rushed out of the cabin and watched a Cessna fly up the valley. It landed on the lake, using only a short section of our hard-won runway.

"If we'd known you only needed a hundred yards, we wouldn't have snowshoed a quarter-mile strip," I said with a grin as the pilot climbed out of the plane.

"I was going to airdrop the box without even landing— but I brought fresh veggies and I thought you'd like to toss your own salad," he replied, hauling out a box overflowing with fruits, vegetables, letters and parcels.

"Oranges . . . apples . . . chocolate bars . . . ," I recited as I looked greedily into the box. "Thanks—you don't know what these mean to us!"

"Oh yes I do," the pilot smiled. "You should see the look on your face. Sorry I can't stay for the party, but I've got more stops to make on my way home." He was shouting over the sound of the engine as he climbed back into the plane.

"This is just like a second Christmas," Sally said, rifling through the box I was carrying as we walked across the lake.

Once inside the cabin, we again sorted our mail by postmark dates before opening it. My parents had asked Ron to forward our mail to this pilot, and we received letters and cards from friends and family dated back to November.

"I think our letters home must have conveyed our craving for sweets," I said when I opened a box which contained a supply of film packed carefully among bags of wrapped candies. Another box was filled with ski waxes, more candies, chocolates, and a note from my parents that read, "Put away your stale old dried fruit. Tonight you can really satisfy your sweet tooth!"

The cabin floor became littered with candy wrappers,

orange peels, and envelopes. We savoured the rare treats, then enjoyed a supper of the first salad we had eaten in almost eight months.

With our supply of film replenished, we were eager to photograph more wildlife and the changing scenery. During the next weeks we enjoyed many days of clear mild weather; days of blue sky and red sunburned noses, glacier goggles, suncream and shirtsleeves. My log book for April twenty-seventh describes a typical day: "Another sunny day! We feel compelled to ski while the snow and weather are good—today we headed up to Ptarmigan Ridge and had a great run down the west side. . . . "

Many mornings our skis clattered on the icy crust of snow as we travelled across Hottah Lake, but within an hour the snow softened as the air warmed to shirtsleeve temperatures. We often skied up to the mountains where the snow was still firm, and I remember one particularly exhilarating descent.

"This is going to be a great run!" Sally exclaimed as we donned what she referred to as our "wipeout gear" of snowpants, parka and gloves. Already my heart was beating wildly in anticipation of the roller-coaster descent as we tightened our boots, buckled down our bindings and fastened safety straps.

We pushed off and were soon flying over mounds and moguls, turning between bumps and boulders, ducking under low branches, and skidding around sharp corners. In ten action-packed minutes we skied down a slope that had taken over an hour to climb.

In the shade the snow was firm, but on the open lower slopes it had turned to a heavy mush in the afternoon sun, and it was difficult to carve telemark and parallel turns. Then Sally executed one of her cross-the-tips-and-tumble-down-the-hill snowplow turns as she fought the heavy snow. In the midst of this spectacular manoeuvre we heard a loud snap. Sally felt a sharp crack and fell.

"Are you all right?" I anxiously called down to Sally as she lay in the snow.

"No!" Sally grimaced. "I think I broke my left . . . ski!"

Fortunately, we always carried a plastic ski tip among the emergency supplies in our packs and were able to temporarily repair the broken ski. The ski was functional, but short and clumsy; it took twice as long to shuffle back to the cabin as it would have with good skis.

"Well, at least you waited until the end of ski season to break a ski," I consoled her.

In early May our ski trips were limited to the mornings. By the afternoons, even the snow high on the mountains had softened to the consistency of mashed potatoes, and the distant rumbling of avalanches warned of danger on the high slopes.

As the days grew warmer, the winged tide of birds began to flow north for the summer. The air was again filled with a medley of birdsong, from the sharp *kiki-kiki* of the lesser yellowlegs to the hoarse two-syllable *haronk* of Canada geese. For Sally and me the sound of geese, more than anything else, signalled that spring had arrived in the north.

It was wonderful to be a part of a northern spring. Each day brought new birds to the valley; we welcomed green-winged teals, harlequin ducks and a host of other feathered visitors. For us, spring was one of nature's most dramatic and colourful spectacles, as birds and animals returned to the valley, red buds blossomed on the birch shrubs, and the first yellow flowers poked through the snow.

The ice on the rivers began to melt, and iridescent green water flooded over the ice. Large pools of water formed in the lowlands and the lake began to flood outward from the shore, tinted by rusty-brown water which seeped from the earth. By the middle of May, melting rains of spring had soaked into the snow, transforming it into a soggy mush.

"This is like wading through oatmeal," I groaned as we tried to ski through the slush one morning. After only a few hundred yards I turned back to the cabin, frustrated at being cabin-bound again when we least expected it.

For a period of two weeks we were "slushed-in." Cold rain pelted down on the soggy snow and an occasional snowstorm swirled feebly through the valley. Even on days when the weather was fair we couldn't travel by ski or snowshoe; we would sink to our knees in the heavy, wet mush. Moving about was almost impossible.

"What do you want to do today?" Sally asked listlessly after four days of sitting around the cabin. "I've read most of

the books, I refuse to play crib, and we can't go anywhere!"
Sally was suffering from the classic symptoms of spring
fever—irritability, lethargy, and mild depression. I decided
the only cure was to busy ourselves with chores around the
cabin.
"I think we should clean out the stovepipes," I suggested.
"We've been putting that off for weeks."
Cleaning the stovepipes was a messy, difficult job, but it
was just the diversion we needed. Burning green wood in the
stove caused thick soot to coat the inside of the pipes; this
soot could catch fire if not cleaned out regularly. We
climbed up onto the roof of the cabin and spent the morning
dismantling the stovepipes, then scrubbed the insides with a
brush. By the time we finished, we were black from head to
toe.
"Now I feel better," Sally said as she wiped a grimy hand
across her forehead. "While we're up here, why don't we
chop the ice off the roof."
For the next two hours, we hacked and shovelled the
heavy water-soaked snow and ice from the eaves. Next, I removed the blurry sheets of plastic which insulated the
windows, and Sally scrubbed the inside walls. Instantly, the
cabin was brighter and more cheerful.
The next day we discovered another project, which ur-
gently needed attending to. Our moose meat had begun to
thaw, even though it was stored under the snow in buckets.
Fearing the sudden spoilage of our meat supply, we
thumbed through our "how-to" books for a recipe for moose
jerky. We cut the meat into long strips, soaked the pieces in
hot brine, then lay them on a rack to drain.
"It looks and smells like Paul's cabin in here," Sally commented after we had strung the strips of meat back and forth
across the warm rafters of the cabin to dry. For five days we
were assailed by the sharp aroma of curing moose meat.
Gradually, the meat dried to a dark, hard jerky. Raw, the
jerky was tough and unappetizing, but we found it to be
tasty when cooked in stews.
Scraps of meat brought many birds and animals to the
cabin, and our favourite visitor was the dark marten we
called Blackie. I looked up from writing one evening to see
Blackie's small face peering around the corner of the

door—two sparkling eyes, long whiskers, and a wet, black nose.

"Come on in," I whispered encouragingly.

The marten slowly stepped into the cabin, looking, listening, and smelling his way around. Sally gasped when he hopped onto the front counter and did a dance on her sketch pad, leaving muddy footprints across the white page. Then he pranced along the side counter, under the bed and into the kitchen area. Ah, the kitchen! Blackie stood up on his rear legs and sniffed the aroma of fresh bread, moose stew and other savoury delights. What is this, a piece of cheese? A mousetrap! I quickly intervened by stamping my foot and the mischievous marten ran out the door.

Blackie became tamer each day until he would take small scraps from our fingers and lick jam from our hands. His tonque was rough, but he was as gentle as a kitten, carefully taking pieces of meat without biting our fingers. It was exciting to have a wild animal trust us enough to feed from our hands. A smaller female marten was also a frequent visitor but never became as tame or gentle as Blackie. Her nervous behavior inspired Sally to name her Spooky.

One morning, we were wakened by a strange noise coming from under the floorboards near our bed. *Meep...Meep...Meep.*

"If that's a mouse, it must be huge!" Sally mused.

We peered through the floorboards, but could see nothing. Behind our cabin, however, we found a small hole tunnelled under the base log. After a few minutes a familiar face appeared at the opening. Spooky! As we were wondering why the marten had tunnelled under the cabin, we heard the meeping sound again.

"Babies!" Sally said. "I'd say that's a good place for a den—it's warm and dry, and even has food delivered right through the cracks."

Later that day the mother marten proudly brought two babies to the front of the cabin, where they tussled and tumbled like kittens. They were curious, clumsy creatures, who spent most of their time with their mother. But after watching Blackie feed freely from our hands, they cautiously approached us for handouts. One baby copied its mother's quick nervous actions, but the other emulated

190

Spring breakup!

A willow ptarmigan

Blackie—a friendly pine marten

Blackie and calmly allowed us to pet him and stroke his chin.

Even with animal visitors to entertain us, we became impatient for the lake to break up. Each morning we walked down to the lake to see if the ice was beginning to crack. Very slowly, the ice turned grey and began to honeycomb into long vertical shards. Although the days were warm, the temperature still fell below freezing at night, and new panes of ice skimmed over the open water.

The remaining snow was no longer the soft, white blanket of winter; it had changed to a coarse, grey corn snow. Under each pine tree where the squirrels and birds had been feeding, the snow was littered with a brown mat of pine cone scales, bark, twigs, and broken buds. Bare ground showed around many trees and south-facing slopes, but in the forest the snow was still over two feet deep.

Our frustration mounted as May slowly melted into June. Then one morning in early June, Sally called me to the lake.

"Breakup!" she shouted excitedly.

We stood on the beach, then stepped cautiously back and watched in amazement as the huge sheet of brittle ice that spanned the lake was pushed against the shore by the wind. Slowly, the grinding, protesting ice was driven onto the shoreline in great piles of jagged, broken crystals; the noise was like a thousand dinner plates being broken. We watched in awe as the mass crept up the beach, crashing and crunching on the rocks, scarring trees as it continued up the shore.

The lake continued to break up for the next five days. But when we woke on June the tenth, the only noise from the lake was a chime-like tinkling. We walked down to the lakeshore and watched waves gently lapping the last fragile fragments of ice.

"Finally!" Sally said, heaving a chunk of ice into the forest. The lake had been ice-covered for more than seven months and we were delighted to see open water again. For Sally and me, the last day of breakup signalled the arrival of a new season in the north.

"Dig the canoe out from under the snow. . . . Summer's here!" I whooped.

CHAPTER 22

Our Second Summer

The morning after breakup, we slid our canoe onto Hottah Lake. As Sally and I canoed along the shoreline our paddles dipped rhythmically, almost noiselessly, into the water.

It felt good to swing a paddle again, and I smiled with contentment as the haunting call of a loon echoed across the still water. "This is my favourite season," I said.

"You said that about autumn . . . and late winter!" Sally laughed.

After months of white silence, we revelled in the new sights, sounds, and scents of spring melting into summer. Reflections were again mirrored on open water, and the shoreline passed by in a blur of colours: yellow buttercups, green moss, and white patches where snow still lingered. We stopped to savour the fragrance of violets and globeflowers in bloom along the water's edge. A medley of new birdsong from the forest mingled with the whispering of wind in the trees and the trickling of water between boulders.

We canoed across the lake and through the marsh to Intermittent Creek. A flock of green-winged teal scooted ahead of the canoe. Further on, a barely audible cheeping caught our attention. Without having to say a word, we turned the canoe towards shore, and went to investigate the sound, walking stealthily through the tall grass.

"Watch we don't step on it—whatever it is!" Sally whispered. Dropping to our knees, we parted the grass and slowly crawled towards the sound. Suddenly, a tiny, brown chick emerged from the grass and ran straight towards us. As I leaned closer with the camera, the sparrow opened its beak and cheeped loudly, expecting to be fed. I took a few photographs and the sparrow hopped closer. Much to my surprise, it climbed onto my shoe. I let the tiny chick rest for a moment, then rolled my foot sideways so that it would climb down. We left quickly then, and canoed away so that the chick's mother could return in peace.

"Why didn't we hear or see as many birds last summer?" I wondered aloud as I pointed to a thrush balancing on a willow branch.

Sally stopped paddling and thought for a moment. "I don't think we had learned to," she replied.

Sally and I had experienced a wonderful awakening of the senses—we noticed details that had escaped our observation during our first summer: new flowers, a different birdsong, and fresh tracks in the soil. We had become attuned to the natural world around us, to the ebb and flow of each season.

One evening as we sat on the doorstep of the cabin, a moose with a familiar-looking scar on its rump splashed along the shore, then stopped directly in front of us. It was the young bull we had seen last summer. Did he recognize us, I wondered.

It looked as though he had been through a hard winter; his ribs were clearly outlined against the tattered remnants of his winter coat. As I watched the young bull I no longer saw just a wild animal standing in the water. I felt a certain kinship with the moose, an understanding of his life in the wilderness. The moose seemed more mature now, more aware of his surroundings. We too were a little older and wiser; we had survived the same long, cold winter, similar hardships, and had struggled through the same soft snow of late spring.

The moose studied us for many minutes with his nose to the air and ears twitching back and forth before he slowly wandered down the shore. "That was like a visit from an old friend," Sally said, then quietly closed the door.

We spent the last two weeks of June re-acquainting ourselves with the lakes and rivers in our domain. Early morning was our favourite time of day for canoeing; the light was at its best for photography and the birds and animals were often feeding. By mid morning, when the birds in the marsh were less active, we would beach our canoe and wander through the woods. Unlike the previous summer when we were busy building the cabin, Sally and I now had the freedom to enjoy the scents and scenes of our valley.

Warmer weather during late June brought back the mosquitoes, forcing us to don headnets and bug jackets, and to splash on our summer cologne of *eau de repellant*. But the mosquitoes were not all bad; they attracted hungry trout to the surface of the lake, where we waited, fishing lines ready.

As we paddled home with our first trout of the season, my mouth watered at the thought of this welcome change—I was tired of freeze-dried burger and moosemeat. "This is going to be great!" I enthused.

For the next four days we ate trout fried, baked, or poached; for breakfast, lunch and supper. But ten trout meals later it was not quite as popular.

"That's enough!" I resisted when Sally suggested fish patties. "How about some moose jerky?"

By July the upper slopes were free of snow and we were able to hike to the high country again. We spent almost the entire month wandering up mountains and through valleys, photographing wildlife and scenery. Sally and I were like two gypsies, living from our backpacks, camping in our small nylon tent, and bathing in icy creeks. We cooked our meals over open campfires, and our clothes acquired the essence of smoke and mosquito repellant. We would return to the cabin just long enough between trips to wash our clothes, to mend our equipment and to pack food for the next expedition.

One of our longest trips was a seven-day trek in search of caribou. We hiked towards Gray Lake, then stumbled across a dusty caribou trail which led towards a valley we had not yet explored. The trail wound through the forest, and down to the valley floor where it was worn into a deep muddy trough from generations of passing caribou. As the valley became wetter and muddier, the main trail fanned out to numerous thin paths which became difficult to follow.

It began raining on the third day, but we plodded on. We hoped that, if the caribou were in the valley, the patter of rain and dripping bushes would cover up the sound of our footsteps and let us get close to the animals. For two more days we followed the paths through swamps, across creeks, and up the side of a mountain without spotting a single caribou. We cursed the rain, shivered through icy creek crossings, and swore at the swamps. Mile after mile went by with no sign of our quarry except mudbaths, split-hooved tracks, and neat piles of pellets.

"We have to head back tomorrow," Sally reminded me as we set up another camp in the rain. "We're just about out of food."

I was disappointed. This was our last chance to photograph caribou before we had to leave Hottah Lake. When we finally turned back, it was with the realization that our fourteen-month stay was not long enough to let us experience everything. We had prearranged with Ron to have our gear flown out on the first of August. We wished that we could stay longer—even just a week or two—but without a radio there was no way to change the date.

When we returned to the cabin, I crossed July twenty-sixth off the calendar. We had only four days left. Sally and I took a farewell trip up the ridge behind our cabin—this was our final opportunity to share an eagle's eye view of our valley.

We made our way up the mountain slowly, stopping often to look down on Hottah Lake.

"Remember how difficult it was to find our way last summer?" Sally asked.

I remembered. Even though we had come to know the game trail along the ridge like a back yard, we still felt the same excitement, the same "mountain high" as we had last summer climbing up for our first view of the valley.

Remnants of snow still lingered in the hollows, flanked

196

by natural gardens of avalanche lilies and mountain blue-bells. Slush showered from our boots as we kicked steps up a steep snow-filled gulley.

"I'm hot," Sally said when we reached the top of the gulley, "Let's take a last roll in the snow!" I needed no more prompting than that. We stripped off our clothes, then rolled naked in the snow to cool down, laughing and hollering from the shock of the cold.

A sharp, high-pitched whistle made us stop and look around—someone, or something, was watching our antics. I scanned the slope and soon spotted the voyeur. A marmot was sitting on a large rock, enjoying the sunshine. In fact, there were marmots all around us.

We dressed quickly, grabbed our cameras, and walked towards the nearest group of marmots. As we approached, each animal turned and scampered into its tunnel.

After a few minutes two young marmots appeared at the entrance of a den, and played in front of us. Their paws were remarkably human-like: long, deft fingers pulled, poked and stroked each other. The marmots wrestled and tumbled, totally unconcerned about our presence. When they finally moved back to their tunnel, Sally and I followed, crawling to the entrance and peering in. Soon one face, then another, appeared at the opening, only a foot away from our cameras!

As we lay in the dirt I took several photographs, then looked over to Sally. Gently, she handed a blade of grass to a young marmot, who grasped it with tiny paws and began to nibble on the delicacy. Sally was smiling with contentment, the edges of her eyes crinkling with happiness. The young marmots' acceptance of us meant that we were no longer intruders, but were a part of their wilderness. We left the marmots in peace and began our hike home.

The next day we began packing. The chainsaw and chisels with which we had hewn our wilderness home were packed first. The axes that had served us so well were next. The handles had never broken, although our bush axe was taped like a wounded soldier.

I laughed when I placed the peavy with the other tools. "Remember dropping this into the icy lake?" I asked Sally.

"And remember wearing these silly things?" Sally

To the high country

Dancing marmots

We felt like gypsies...

smiled as she held up one of the down-filled face masks we had worn when the temperature was forty-five below.

"This made a pretty good washing machine after all," I said, packing away the toilet plunger.

Events flooded back, as if being replayed in a movie. . . . We talked of our first night at Hottah Lake and of the moose that had come to our tent. We reminisced about learning to cut notches for the cabin, washing our faces in the rusty gold pan, and about the morning ritual of lighting our wood-burning stove during the long winter months.

"I'm going to miss this place—even the rainy days," Sally said quietly, her eyes misting over.

"Me too, but I kind of look forward to getting back to Vancouver," I answered unconvincingly. I was having trouble with my voice.

Our life would certainly be different when we returned to civilization. Back in the city, we would have to mind our manners. No more fishing flies out of our tea with our fingers or wearing bug-hats at the dinner table. Serving meals out of aluminum camp pots and sitting on the ground would no longer be appropriate. Tossing the dregs of camp coffee from our cups out the door, and sweeping crumbs between the floorboards for our pet martens would have to stop. . . . Come to think of it, having pet martens wouldn't be very acceptable either.

On our last night in the cabin, we read through our journals, sharing our thoughts and feelings of the past fourteen months. We talked about returning to the city, and more importantly, about how we would get there. We had wanted to canoe from Hottah Lake down the Tucho, Pitman and Stikine rivers back to the gravel road heading south. But we had studied the Tucho River through binoculars from Skyline Ridge and had discovered that it was not navigable; after the first mile, rocks and rapids stretched as far as we could see. Even portaging the canoe was impossible, as steep cliffs and impenetrable forest lined the river.

We had developed a respect for the power of these wild northern rivers, and we now realized that even the Pitman and Stikine rivers would tax our canoeing abilities to their limit. Still, we couldn't just be whisked back to Iskut in a winged machine. We needed time to adjust. We decided to be flown to the Pitman River, and to canoe from there under our own steam.

The next morning, Sally and I waited nervously, sitting beside our pile of gear on the beach and listening for the far-off thrumming sound that would mean a plane was on its way. Would the pilot remember the August first appointment we had made eleven months earlier? Was it August first, or had we gained a day, or even more, on our calendar? Would he fly in this day, or the next?

Around noon we heard the droning of an aircraft. The plane circled the lake twice, then landed and taxied to shore. An unfamiliar pilot stepped out.

"Ron couldn't make it, but I came for you instead," he said. "I'm Murray."

After helping him load our gear into the plane, Sally and I walked up the winding path to our cabin to say one last farewell.

"Perhaps one day our cabin will be a shelter for a pilot in need," I said to Sally as we stood holding hands. We had left the cabin stocked with food, some fuel and first aid supplies, even though there would be few visitors in this remote location.

I shuttered the windows, and then we went to the front door for a final glance inside. We heard a rustle from a dark corner at the back of the cabin. After a moment, our favourite marten peered around the bed frame, mischievously looked at us, and slowly padded out of the cabin then into the forest.

"Goodbye Blackie . . . ," Sally whispered softly.

CHAPTER 23

Canoeing the Stikine

Our cabin grew smaller as the plane taxied down the lake. Once we became airborne I looked back wistfully, unable to tear my eyes away. Sally looked back only briefly, then steadfastly fixed her gaze forward.

"You sure you don't want to fly all the way to Iskut?" the pilot asked. "It would be easier."

"No . . . we need time," I replied slowly.

He seemed to understand our mood and nodded his acknowledgment. Five minutes later, we descended to the Pitman River. I tensed as trees and shoreline passed by in a blur, then breathed a sigh of relief when the noisy aircraft finally came to a stop at a sandbar.

I jumped out and held onto the plane to prevent it from drifting downstream while Sally and the pilot unloaded our canoe and packs.

"When do you think you'll get to Iskut?" Murray asked as he climbed back into the plane.

"Oh, six or seven days . . . or maybe eight," I replied.

"O.K." he said cheerfully. "See you when you get there —and not a day sooner."

After the plane took off, we climbed into our canoe. We still hadn't felt the full impact of leaving Hottah Lake—it seemed we were just on another canoe trip down another river.

Although we had expected a difficult journey, our first day on the river was quiet, almost peaceful. We encountered only a few rolling waves, a hint of whitewater. But our second day brought greater challenges. The canoe bobbed wildly down a series of small rapids, glanced off a few boulders, and took on water as waves crashed over the bow. The current flowed even swifter and more turbulent when we joined the Stikine River.

The Tahltan Indians call the Stikine the "Wild River," and we soon learned why. Only half a mile downstream from the junction of the Stikine, we approached Shreiber Canyon and prepared to run our first large rapids.

"Left!" I yelled as water surged over the bow, drenching Sally.

"Draw, Draw!" I bellowed as we guided the canoe through the rapids, just missing a pile of boulders. We were planning, paddling, prying, panting, shouting and fighting the current every minute. By the time we reached smoother water we were soaking wet and feeling weak, but we were grinning from ear to ear.

We pulled the canoe into an eddy behind a large boulder and rested for a few minutes. We had managed to keep the canoe pointing the right way, and most of the water was still in the river, where it belonged. But the run through the rapids had tested the limits of our canoeing skills—and even worse stretches of water lay ahead.

With each additional river that drained from the high mountains, the Stikine ran wilder. The canoeing was fast and furious as we rushed through narrow channels, swift boulder-strewn passages, whitewater, and standing waves. In the calmer water between rapids we had time to build up our courage for the next rough water.

"Looks as though the biggest rapids—at Goat Canyon—are just ahead!" I commented, referring to our waterproof map.

We pulled the canoe out and walked down the shoreline to survey the river. Around the corner was Goat Canyon—a narrow chute of roaring, white turbulence. From the right bank, Beggarly Creek rushed in, creating high waves for added excitement.

This was the section we had been most worried about, but it didn't appear to be as wicked as I had expected. "Looks pretty wild," I said. "But if we run the left side, cross over below that big rock, then power through the...."

"What do you mean, 'WE'?" Sally interrupted. "I vote we portage around the chute."

After a brief discussion of the merits of canoeing solo, I agreed to the portage. We spent half a day carrying our gear across the waist-deep, icy water of Beggarly Creek, and hauling the canoe across with ropes. Then we went overland for three hundred yards, carrying the canoe and packs over a steep rocky route before returning to the Stikine.

After Goat Canyon we encountered only one more difficult section. It was a deep, unnamed canyon, where waves surged against sheer cliffs.

"Yeeeeeh-Haaaw!" I yelled as the canoe crashed through the first foaming wave. I dropped to my knees for better balance as swells, jets, and huge waves of icy water exploded all around us. It was like riding a bucking bronco through a water trough. With stout paddles, straining muscles, and split-second panic we blasted through the maelstrom, then shot out into the bright sunlight again, whooping and hollering.

Another mile downriver the Stikine became broader and quieter, and the river valley changed from tall spruce forests to smaller birch and pine. We stopped to pick the wild strawberries and raspberries along the shoreline, and enjoyed the river's slower pace.

On the morning of our fifth day, we saw the first signs of civilization—an old log cabin which stood facing the river. A few miles further, another abandoned cabin sat proudly on a small isolated homestead. We continued down the river and by late afternoon we were within ten miles from the end of our journey. Although we could have canoed out that day something inside me held me back.

"Let's camp on the river tonight," I said to Sally. "I'm still in no hurry."

We set up our tent on the sandy shore near a grove of

pine trees. Moose tracks led to the river and raccoon prints followed the shoreline. As twilight descended on our quiet camp, the small fire snapped and crackled, sending up a spray of sparks, and fingers of orange light cast a warm glow into the surrounding shadows.

We felt soothed by the faint glowing stars, the scent of wildflowers, and the soft whisper of the wind. Once more I recalled words of Thoreau: "We need the tonic of wildness. We can never have enough of nature. We must be refreshed by the sight of inexhaustible vigor, vast and titanic features, and wilderness with its living and decaying trees, the thunder cloud, and the rain which lasts three weeks and produces freshets. We need to witness our own limits transgressed, and some life pasturing freely where we never wander."

Sally and I sat close to the fire and quietly talked about returning to civilization the next day.

"You know, we are luckier than most people," I said, holding her tightly. "We've shared a natural world that few people have ever seen. I'll always remember the slower, quieter days at Hottah lake."

That night around the campfire was the end of a wonderful adventure. We were leaving the next day, but we both knew in our hearts that it would be only a short time before we would again need the "tonic of wildness" to revive our senses and souls.

CHAPTER 24

Epilogue

Sally and I pulled our canoe out of the Stikine River where it met the gravel road leading to Iskut. We stacked our canoe, packs and paddles at the edge of the roadway, then stuck out our thumbs for a ride. Within an hour a pickup truck stopped for us and our gear.

"Been camping?" the bearded driver asked, as we drove away.

"Well . . . sort of," I answered. "For fourteen months."

"It's 'bout an hour to Iskut," he said with a grin. "You can tell me all about it."

The old truck bumped and rattled over the road as we told our story. We were travelling only twenty-five miles an hour, but even that seemed too fast, and we gripped the seat nervously. I talked faster and louder when the truck gained momentum going down hills.

"That was a good story—maybe you should write a book," the man said as we unloaded at Iskut. He gave me a hearty slap on the back that sent me reeling, then climbed in the truck and rattled down the road, leaving us in a cloud of dust.

That evening we enjoyed the first hamburgers and fries that we had tasted in fourteen months. We shared a glass of beer, which promptly made us giddy. Showers, hot water from taps, and indoor washrooms were fascinating to us. Lights that came on at the flick of a switch, and a laundry machine that didn't look like a bucket and toilet plunger were downright novelties.

We stayed at Iskut for a day, gradually re-acquainting ourselves with people and plumbing. Then, we cautiously started our truck and drove south—slowly. Northern villages gave way to larger towns, then to busier cities on our way to Vancouver. The pace of traffic became faster and louder. The speeds made us dizzier each day.

Our return to civilization was almost too much; from fireweed to firetrucks, trout to traffic, and the cabin to convenience stores. Some changes were easier to accept than others: hamburgers, beer and ice cream were ones we quickly adjusted to. In fact, it seemed to me that we stopped at every ice cream and fruit stand that we spotted on the drive home. It was more difficult to adjust to the fast pace of cars and people, and to the steady noise of the city.

Sally and I have found that we now look at the world from a different perspective. The wilderness has taught us new values. We often stop to smell the fragrance of a flower or listen to a bird sing while the rest of the city rushes past us. We had expected to return to nine-to-five jobs and pick up where we left off, but life in the wild has pointed us in new directions. We now devote our time to teaching cross-country skiing and photography, to writing books and articles, and to sharing our adventure with others through slide presentations and lectures.

Through our writing, lectures, and photography, we keep our experiences alive and teach the value and beauty of the wild north country. Sally and I had seen—and lived—a lifestyle that past generations knew, but which future generations may never get to sample. Not unless we take care to preserve some of our natural heritage.

We have come to realize that the value of the wilderness cannot be measured by board-feet of lumber, tons of coal, or megawatts of power. Industry cannot replace an alpine meadow of wildflowers once an open pit mine has scarred the land, or return a river to its natural state once a dam has flooded a valley. Man must learn that some land needs to be left on which the moose can browse, the grizzly bear can roam freely, and where other wildlife can live undisturbed.

Sally and I have gradually acclimatized to the city, but we often think of our encounters with wild animals, and of our rustic log cabin on the shore of Hottah Lake.

"Would you do it again?" is a question people often ask.

Our answer is always an emphatic, "YES!" Despite some hardships and discomforts, we found a life that was peaceful, rewarding, and simple. We learned that we could depend on each other, that we could handle almost any task we set for ourselves, and that it is possible to make dreams come true.

I often recall Sally's words as we sat around the campfire during our last night in the wilderness.

"This is where we belong," she had said quietly.

Those words summed up our reasons for going to the wilderness, and the reason we will some day return.